Music Therapy in Special Education

(restriction good for 1 month only)

M.T.

① play ex of music
(Music T. in special ed.
Tues ② Reading pp 31-46
③ play folk song
④ Bring blank tape

MUSIC THERAPY  IN SPECIAL EDUCATION

PAUL NORDOFF
CLIVE ROBBINS

Second Edition
Revised by Clive Robbins

MMB
MMB MUSIC, INC.

MUSIC THERAPY IN SPECIAL EDUCATION
Second Edition – revised by Clive Robbins
Paul Nordoff and Clive Robbins

Printer: Cushing-Malloy, Inc., Ann Arbor, Michigan
Third printing: September, 1995
PRINTED IN USA
ISBN: 0-918812-22-4

For further information and catalogs, contact:

MMB Music, Inc.
Contemporary Arts Building
3526 Washington Avenue
Saint Louis, MO 63103-1019

Phone: 314 531-9635; 800 543-3771 (USA/Canada)
Fax: 314 531-8384

To Mummy and Hep
for the best reasons in the world

*Music is a moral law. It gives a soul to the universe,
wings to the mind, flight to the imagination,
a charm to sadness, and life to everything.*

PLATO

Contents

Foreword

When I was invited to write a foreword for this remarkable book I accepted with pleasure. After such alacrity, however, I wondered if I could perform the task. The book is a teaching book. But can two such inspiring performers as Paul Nordoff and Clive Robbins tell anyone else "how to do it"? Indeed, can any others, save these two, so combine their talents as to make an inspired whole?

I am no stranger to the work of these two men. Dr. Nordoff is one of our best composers. In Clive Robbins he has found an able and dedicated partner. Years ago they visited me in my home to share with me their dawning concept of the inestimable value of music in the teaching and development of retarded minds and closed personalities. A lover of music myself and already aware of its power, at once healing and stimulating, I was swept by their understanding of this power and its practical use. Since then I have heard of the increasing success of their work, have met with them from time to time, have corresponded.

Now their book is finished. I confess I opened the manuscript with trepidation. How could the writers impart to readers their own inspiration, their own dedication? Doubting, I read; and now, having read, I report that somehow they have done it. There is a true, living quality in these pages. Let music *live,* they insist. Only live music can be projected and transmitted. For the musically proficient as well as for the teacher less experienced in group musical activity who wants to deepen and develop her work, their instruction is clear and to the point.

The value of various instruments is described imaginatively and with brilliance. The use of contrast, of inventiveness, in both music and instrument is profoundly exciting. Rhythm, too, is necessary but must not be monotonous lest it lull instead of invite. Music for the slow mind of the retarded should in theme be simple, expressive, strong, basic. It should be played without sentiment but with meaning and control. Applause, too, should be purposeful and controlled and not just romping noise.

Whether they are showing how to strengthen a speech-handicapped child's efforts through song, how to focus concentration in a working game, or how to structure and enliven a children's play with music, the authors stress the limitless potentials of music, first to activate and then to support and enrich.

In large and in detail, these two superb teachers are teaching others to do what they do, and that is how to use music to open the closed mind, to stimulate the withdrawn personality, and gently to bring the lost child into the living world.

In short, the writers, out of their creative experience, have written a beautiful, practical book. I am glad to endorse it.

Pearl S. Buck

Acknowledgments

We wish to express our appreciation to: the directors and staff of Sunfield Children's Home, Clent, England, who provided the situation and the opportunities for the first realizations of this work while inspiring us with their high standards of educational therapy—particularly by their creative use of plays with children. Frau Dr. Erlacher, Heidenheim, for her stimulating production of "The Other Wise Man," and Dr. and Mrs. Martin F. Palmer, for the encouragement they gave to our development of this play with children at the Institute of Logopedics, Wichita. We remember Dr. Palmer with warm gratitude.

The very many associates in the School District of Philadelphia, Pennsylvania: Mrs. Elizabeth Greenfield and other members of the Board for endorsing the music therapy program for trainable childen; Associate Superintendents past and present, Dr. Helen C. Bailey and Mr. John B. Taulane, who took the initiative of founding the program, Robert C. Taber and David Horowitz for their firm support; Dr. Ernest Kohl, Superintendent of District 6; Mr. Robert Stewart and all the principals of trainable centers; the teachers of the trainable classes throughout the city for their collaboration, particularly Thomasina Amos, Lee Beinstein, Mary Drosey, Mildred Kirkland, Edith Morrell, Elmira Sirbaugh, and Claire Robinson, matron of the Joseph E. Hill School, Germantown, Pennsylvania, 1962–66; Hope Elizabeth Allen for her imaginative support of a project with educable girls.

The Philadelphia Foundation for funding the filming of trainable children in music therapy.

Dr. Helen C. Hosmer for initiating workshops in music therapy at the Crane Department of Music, State University College, Potsdam, New York.

Stephen Portmann and Jaakko Jylha, who arranged the music therapy training and demonstration project in Finland, and Delores Di Paola and Peter Strong of the American-Scandinavian Foundation, who extended it through all the Scandinavian countries.

The van Ameringen Foundation, which supported the Scandinavian project and the writing of this book, especially Mrs. Douglas Auchincloss and Joan A. Strober. For the same reasons, our lasting thanks to Miss Katharine·Cornell.

Dr. Oiva Ollila, Sister Gunnel Stenbeck, and Tuulikki Hjelt for the warmth of welcome and hospitality that "Rinnekoti" gave to music therapy and us; also for spurring the completion of three chapters of this book for Finnish translation. Mirja Lavanne, who translated these and transmitted music therapy instruction in "Suomi."

Our Danish colleagues, for the stimulating quality of their interest and for the opportunities they gave us—notably Sven Brandt, M.D., and the kindergarten staff of the Cerebral Palsy and Child Neurology Clinic; Poul Nilsson and friends on the staff of Geelsgaard Kostskole; and Inge Nilsson, Speech Consultant, Ministry of Education, Copenhagen. Karen M. Ahlmann-Ohlsen, Else Østbirk, and Sonja Bundgaard-Nielsen of the Danmark-Amerika Fondet for willing, friendly assistance at every turn. The George C. Marshall Memorial Fund In Denmark for its financial support.

Brewster Miller, M.D., for scheduling an experimental demonstration of music therapy at the Eleventh World Congress of the International Society for Rehabilitation of the Disabled; and Dr. Mary O'Donnel and her staff at St. Brendan's Day Clinic for Spastic Children, Dublin, for wholeheartedly cooperating in its realization.

The Foundation for Arts and Letters, in Memory of Rudolf Steiner, for its continuing support, and the Haas Community Funds, for assisting the development of special instruments.

The Theodore Presser Company for permission to use musical illustrations in the text, and Calvert Bean, Jr., Vice President and Publication Director, for his cordial, practical interest.

Miss Catherine A. English, Associate Professor of Music, and Miss Mary E. English, Professor of Music, Crane Department of Music, State University College, Potsdam, New York; Mabel

14

G. Brown, Dolores F. Cave, and Virginia Zellat, of the Philadelphia Public School System, for reading parts of the manuscript and making helpful suggestions.

Nellie Lee Bok and Beatrice and Bernard J. Garber, for their personal commitment, their never-failing encouragement and guidance.

Herbert and Gail Levin, Vera Moretti and Carol Robbins, music therapists, colleagues in the work, and friends directly associated with its development.

All those who have shared with us the feeling of the importance of music therapy for handicapped children, who have given us their practical support or the strength of their enthusiasm.

PAUL NORDOFF
CLIVE ROBBINS

Introduction

This book originated in a series of manuals compiled for special education teachers in the public schools of Philadelphia, Pennsylvania, and in resource materials prepared for participants in music therapy workshops and seminars given in all five Scandinavian countries under the sponsorship of the American-Scandinavian Foundation, the van Ameringen Foundation, and the Finnish National Welfare Association for the Mentally Deficient.

This revised edition has been prepared for music therapists working in a variety of clinical settings, for public school music teachers working with special classes, for special education teachers who are interested in exploring the possibilities of musical activity for their children and who possess enough skill with an instrument to begin the development of a program, and for any musicians who may find or create opportunities to use their skills for the benefit of handicapped children. Throughout the text, "therapist," "teacher," and "musician" should be read as being interchangeable.

The book was written as a guide and resource manual solely for work with handicapped children. But in its subsequent years of use, many music therapists and teachers, including ourselves, have found that much of its content applies directly to work with adults—widely in the case of the mentally retarded, and to varying extents with the multiply or communicatively handicapped, the psychiatrically hospitalized, and with geriatric patients. In this very diversified field there are marked differences in the needs, abilities, conditions, and situations of the groups who comprise it. Therapists working in these areas also differ in their goals and perspectives, their values, priorities, and musical and material resources. For these reasons it is impossible to be specific, even in the most rudimentary manner, regarding the suitability, *or adaptability*, of materials for particular groups. Most of the principles and considerations of materials, music, musical activity and experience set forth in the various sections stand as relating widely to music therapy with adults—the practical implementation, interpretation, adaptation, and choice of materials belong necessarily to the free judgement of therapists in their working situations.

The work with children has continued to develop since the book's first edition. Our own experience has increased and, again, we have received many helpful suggestions from colleagues and associates. While it has not been necessary to make any revisions that reflect fundamental changes of approach, values or philosophy, a number of technical, practical matters have been updated, principally in *Chapter Three*.

In work with children and adults, the ability to adapt materials successfully to meet the needs and/or abilities of particular groups is an important aspect of music therapy technique. With suitable adaptation, the usefulness and effectiveness of materials are widened considerably—and many materials lend themselves well to adaptation. This subject is addressed in *Appendix 2*.

The techniques and principles of creating developmentally significant experiences in group musical activities are not exclusive to any one group or kind of handicapped children. The divers classifications of special education and the grouping of children under the various specialized treatment disciplines neither create clear-cut boundaries of musical ability nor divide children's qualities of responsiveness into separate categories. Within each group, individual rates of maturation vary widely and spread the age suitability of materials; identically classified groups at different levels of educational activation require different materials. Furthermore, the kinds of musical experience and activity here described possess a universality that carries across educational and rehabilitational divisions.

For this reason we have treated the application of materials broadly, using the term "handicapped" child in all general references. This includes any child whose development is affected to some individual extent by a mental, physical, or emotional dysfunction, or by multiple handicaps. In places we have referred to the "trainable" and the "educable" to indicate more closely

18

the particular sphere of effectiveness of specific materials. These terms also include those children not so categorized but who are functionally or responsively equivalent. Where we use the phrase "young children" we are thinking mainly in terms of chronological age, although flexibly, with reference to ability levels. The practical operational choice of suitability of materials or methods is left throughout to the teacher or therapist to be made with reference to her group.

This book emphasizes the effectiveness of teamwork. When a pianist and leader work closely together, the pianist is able to concentrate fully on the music and on playing perceptively to suit the children's responses to it; the leader gives her entire attention to directing the children's activity so as to realize the musical experiences with all possible vividness and clarity, guiding or encouraging individuals in whatever ways they require. The team members' collaboration is reciprocal, the pianist follows the leader's management of the group, the leader works to maintain the musical connection between children and pianist.

With teamwork of this kind, intensive experiences involving children's participation can be built and sustained. The team can cope resourcefully with exacting circumstances and can manage larger groups effectively; it can also handle the often complicated material side of music therapy with efficiency. Two can share the responsibility and work of arranging the music room for special purposes, preparing and setting out instruments, and also the many preparations necessary in stage work.

The fact that two teachers present songs or activities with equal enthusiasm, sharing the same aims and working in close cooperation, makes its human impression on the children; the materials that are used and the experiences they impart acquire impact and substantiality.

This is not, of course, to say that a person who works alone cannot conduct effective music therapy. On the contrary, a skillful teacher or musician with a direct, personal style can create attractive and therapeutic experiences. Our point is that if she were given the right kind of supportive assistance, she could realize more varied and extensive experiences, engage more severely handicapped children, and integrate more children in a group's activity.

All instructional material relative to making music and handling children, given here for each form of activity, applies to the work of a team and equally to the work of a single musician-teacher.

The present book concentrates entirely on musical activities in a group setting. Although working with individuals within the group is much discussed, the book does not deal in any way directly with clinical individual music therapy as a distinct mode of treatment.[1] A therapist or teacher will find, however, that many of the materials are suitable for individual work and that the greater part of the considerations of music and many principles of practical implementation apply to it.

The treatment of music and the content and handling of group activities in this book have direct application to music education in the regular grades, particularly to musical activities with kindergarten and grades 1 through 4.

One area of music therapy, or music in special education, that has undergone considerable exploration since the present book's first publication is music with hearing impaired children. Although no part of the book was written with hearing impaired children in mind, fully eighty percent of its content was found to apply closely to music with this group. However, a comprehensive music curriculum for the hearing impaired necessitated many additional developments which are documented in *Music for the Hearing Impaired—and Other Special Groups* (see *Appendix* 4). In many ways this book amplifies and extends *Music Therapy in Special Education*, particularly in such areas as advanced instrumental activities, charting and chart reading, music reading, auditory training, and dance and movement. Wherever it could be helpful, specific page references to *Music for the Hearing Impaired—and Other Special Groups* are given in the text.

In several sections of the book we have given abbreviated references to identify the sources of materials being discussed or used for illustration. These sources are all listed in *Appendix* 4, where the abbreviations will be self-explanatory.

[1]For information on this subject see *Creative Music Therapy.*

20

Chapter One

Singing

Group singing provides a range of stimulating, liberating experiences for handicapped children. Each musical attribute or structural characteristic of the songs they sing directly influences the quality and extent of their participation. Melodic color and freshness vitalize their awareness. Harmonies with impact and movement give emotional fiber to their singing experiences. Expressive variety in the rhythmic structures in melody and accompaniment enlivens the words of the songs and, in turn, enlivens the singers. Songs with content they find meaningful are sung with conviction. When words are set to music with the normal emphases and inflections of speech, children are able to sing with natural ease. Melodic lines that have expressive affinity with the meaning of the words increase the directedness of their singing. A comfortable pitch range for their voices maintains participation throughout the song. Tempos that give time for the forming and enunciation of words help them to sing with satisfaction. Musical and meaningful places in melodies for taking breaths will enable them to sing with more verve.

A handicapped child singing intently is deeply committed to his singing. The musical instrument he uses is his own body, his voice, and he experiences his singing as a direct extension of himself. Moment by moment his voice—his most intimate means of self-expression—carries forth, through his singing, his concentration upon· the melody and the words. His memory raises these into consciousness as he sings and, at the same time, he lives in the meaning of what he is singing. Perceptive, cognitive, and expressive capacities are working together. The child's personality becomes integrated in the act of singing and functionally organized by the musical structure and content of the song itself. Suffusing his whole experience, and inseparable from any part of it, are his feelings about the song, about himself singing, and the particular quality of his pleasure in the singing group situation.

Singing can thus be an experience of arousal for the handicapped child, of freedom from many of the confusions and restrictions of pathology. He becomes able to use personal capacities with greater consciousness and can experience, as a result, direct, substantial fulfillment.

This happens to individual children within the group setting. The overall responsiveness of the children, their mutuality of concentration and uplift, supports each individual's personal experiences and gives them a positive social foundation. In this way experiences in group singing can influence the development of social relationships among the children.

Such are the broad effects that singing can have upon handicapped children. Particular results, such as any lessening of behavior disturbances in individuals, the stimulation of speech formation, the overcoming of fearfulness and the like, also become positive factors in the group dynamics and further the cumulative benefit for all.

Choosing Songs

The most effective kinds of songs for handicapped children are those about activities that happen within the songs themselves, or about things or events the children know, or can imagine, or can grow to understand. These songs have a personal reality for them and arouse greater involvement.

Every assembly should open with a "greeting song," for the pleasure it gives creates a mood of active unity in the group.

Example:

Good Morning Song

Boys and girls can sing this song antiphonally, or individual children can sing a phrase, each in turn.

In the classroom, with smaller groups, a song can be used in which each child is greeted by name.

Example:

Greeting Song

Assemblies, or singing sessions in the classroom led by the music teacher or classroom teacher, can include songs on many subjects:

The days of the week
The weather
Counting the number of boys and girls present
Spelling their names
Naming parts of the children's bodies, facial features, hands, fingers, hair, etc.
Naming the children's clothes
Colors
The world around–animals, sun, moon, flowers, trees, etc.
The children's houses
Different kinds of feelings
Play activities
Birthdays
Seasonal or topical celebrations
Personal hygiene
Safety

In many songs the content can be acted or pointed out, or its sense expressed in question-and-answer phrases sung antiphonally between an individual and the group or between boys and girls.

The children must be able to believe in each song they sing and identify not only with its content, but with the words that are used to express it. For this reason songs are less effective if their words are too adult, abstract, cute or affectedly childish, or obviously lacking in sincerity. Words should be simple and forthright; if they are chosen carefully to say what they have to say with clarity of expression, they need not rhyme. This is particularly true if the melodic and rhythmic setting of important words emphasizes their expressive value.

Songs can increase handicapped children's awareness of things or activities.

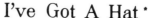

I've Got A Hat *

Briskly (♩ = 128)

1. I've got a hat! I've got a hat! I'll go for a
2. I've got a hat! I've got a hat! I'll go for a

walk, For a walk in the rain. The rain is rain - ing. It's
walk, For a walk in the wind. The wind is blow - ing. It's

* An eye-catching hat is needed which each child can wear as he takes his turn in acting out the song. The acting
can express whatever the child feels about the "weather" in the verses, which can end as follows:
1st Verse- "It's wet!": brushing raindrops off the hat.
2nd Verse- "It's off!": skimming it across the room.
3rd Verse- "It's cold!": pulling it down over the ears.
4th Verse- "It's hot": taking off the hat and using it as a fan.

Songs can be used as teaching aids; these should be authentically musical and hold the possibility for the children to express—or develop—as they sing, a natural interest and pleasure in the subject. Even if a child has not yet understood a song's content, or is only partly comprehending it, his interest will be drawn toward the subject if the music and the words that present it are attractive. Songs as teaching aids should be thought of as ways of bringing delight, play, and, consequently, a heightened interest in learning activities that are so often arduous and routinely repetitive for these children.

I Have A Name *

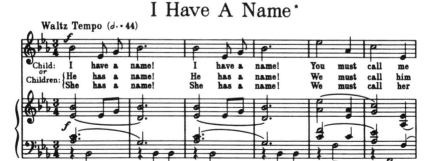

Waltz Tempo (♩. = 44)

Child: I have a name! I have a name! You must call me
or
Children: { He has a name! He has a name! We must call him
{ She has a name! She has a name! We must call her

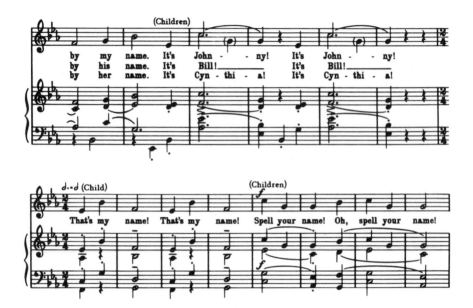

by my name. It's John — ny! It's John — ny!
by his name. It's Bill! It's Bill!
by her name. It's Cyn - thi - a! It's Cyn - thi - a!

That's my name! That's my name! Spell your name! Oh, spell your name!

* The spelling of the name can be done from memory, but it is more fun if the name of the child singing the solo part is written on a blackboard before the song begins. It can be written by the child or by the teacher. After the spelling, the child will enjoy dancing with a classmate to the last phrase of the song.

At the close of a singing session, a "goodbye song" should be sung.

Goodbye!*

Slow March Tempo (♩ = 68)

Good - bye! Good - bye! Oh, thank you and good -

*The names of the children can be added as follows throughout the song:

Good - bye, Sam! Good - bye, Vi - o - let! Oh, thank you

The Setting of Words to Music and the Speech-Handicapped Child

Song and speech are closely related. Most handicapped children are speech-handicapped; many are severely limited in their verbal abilities. Some, through emotional or organic deficits, hardly use verbal communication at all. Singing can stimulate the speech of these children; many teachers and therapists have often heard them attempt to sing words they usually do not or cannot speak. Therefore when we use song with them we should examine how best it can encourage their speech.

The most intimate relationship between sung words and spoken words is the fact that both have (1) tonal inflection and (2) stress-emphasis (accent) upon certain syllables of words and upon particular words in a phrase. In speech these occur spontaneously as part of both the natural order and the expressive use of language. In songs, tonal inflection is given to words through melody, and stress-emphasis through rhythmic accent.

When selecting songs, compare the way in which the words are set to music with their naturally spoken inflections and accents. Unfortunately, in many children's songs, the natural inflections and accents of speech are distorted. These songs cannot give effective help to a handicapped child's speech. His experiences of, and attempts to sing, distorted settings of words can only bring confusion into his limited verbal capacities.

In contrast, a musical setting of words that enhances the natural inflections and accents of speech *adds to their significance and intensifies their expressive value.* For speech-handicapped children this becomes an effective stimulant for participating in singing with greater verbal consciousness—it reinforces their efforts at speech formation.

The following illustrations point out principles in word-setting that can be used as a guide in selecting songs for handicapped children.

Rhythmic Stressing of Syllables

In everyday speech we stress, for example, the second syllable of "re*mem*ber," the first of "*birth*day," the last of "to*day*." Any

27

syllable that is normally stressed in speech should fall on an accented beat of the music:

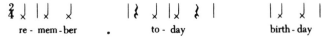

These words are rhythmically distorted if set in the following way:

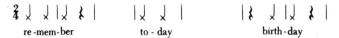

Tonal Settings That Follow Inflections of Speech

We also stress by pitch—the variations in highness and lowness of speaking tone we use in order to express both meaning and feeling. Syllables on which the speaking voice naturally rises should, when sung, be on higher tones than those syllables on which the voice falls.

The settings below do not correspond to the usual speech inflections:

In some songs rhythmic and tonal distortions can be found together:

Verbal Emphasis and Melodic Rhythm

Accented syllables and important one-syllable words may be further stressed by being given a relatively longer time value. This prolongation heightens the meaning of the words and gives rhythmic interest to the melodies of songs.

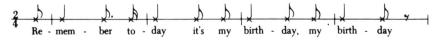

To give these words an appropriate inflection they could be tonally set as follows:

Re - mem - ber   to - day   it's   my   birth - day,   my   birth - day

Speech Phrase and Melodic Phrase

When a speech phrase or a line of a poem is set to music, only those words and accented syllables which are expressively important should be stressed by pitch and/or prolongation. Words of secondary importance and unaccented syllables are given shorter time values and are generally lower in pitch:

Run   in - to   the   cen - ter   clap   your   hands!
Jump in - to   the   cen - ter   stamp your   feet!

The melodic-rhythmic vitality and interest in this song-phrase result from: (1) the length and pitch of the tones on which the important words and accented syllables are sung—"Run" and "Jump," "cen" of "center," "clap" and "stamp," "hands" and "feet," and (2) the shorter time values and lower tones of the unaccented words—"into the," "ter" of "center," "your." (Notice the rest for a breath before the high note on "clap" or "stamp" that this setting provides. Well-placed rests for breathing that occur naturally and expressively facilitate the children's singing.)

The content of speech often expressively modifies the inflection of words and phrases. For example, when asking a question the voice usually rises; in setting this to music, the melody should rise in pitch.

Example:

What Day Is It Today?^{*}

The tempo and dynamics should be suited to the class but should be lively.

What day is it to-day? What day is it to-day? Is it
What day is it to-day? What day is it to-day? Is it

(Shout) (Shout)

Sun - day? No! Is it Sun - day? No!
Mon - day? No! Is it Mon - day? No!

Melodies can carry more dramatic variations of inflection that are expressively true to the mood or character of the statement. For example, in "The Crying Song," the descending octave used in setting "just cry," and the ascending octave of "just sing" express the contrasting moods of the words (See page 36).

These fundamental principles underlie the expressive union of song and speech, a union that is important to the speech-handicapped child. When melody subserves words and emphasizes both their meaning and mood, songs are more naturally singable, their tonal and rhythmic structures more stimulating. It is, however, not always possible to arrive at a perfect marriage of melody and words and one cannot be dogmatic in applying these principles to the selection of material; there are many excellent songs in which the mood or beauty of the melody outweighs an occasionally mis-set word. For example, the setting of the word "chariot" in "Swing Low, Sweet Chariot."

30

Harmony

The harmony in many children's songs consists of two chords—the tonic and the dominant—and possibly a third—the subdominant. The harmonic element of music directly affects our emotions; when it is consistently this restricted the children receive limited musical-emotional experience. This is especially true if the chords are played only in the closed root position. More *open voicings* will add tonal breadth and fullness. These same harmonies can become more dynamic and varied in emotional effect when *inverted*. They then provide harmonic support—yet keep a melody moving by withholding the sense of stable balance the root position triad carries, until this is right for the melody. Many instances of the use of *open voicings* and *inverted triads* will be found in the music illustrating this chapter.

Songs with limited harmonization can be given increased vitality and emotional richness by the addition of *secondary seventh chords*, those on the 1st, 2nd, 3rd, 4th, 6th, and 7th scale tones. These may be used in both root position and inversion.

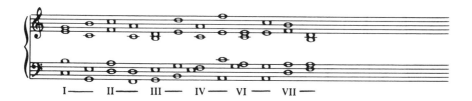

Example:

31

The Emotional Quality of Songs

Almost all retarded children are either emotionally disturbed or emotionally immature. Song can become an effective educator of their emotions. Each song has an emotional content that it can impart to the children who sing it; a variety of songs with many different emotional qualities gives them experiences of a spectrum of emotional life. Songs can arouse children to excitement, gladden them with pleasure, calm them to thoughtfulness. Through the feelings of serene warmth that a song can give, the children's consciousness can be deepened and stabilized. Such a variety of emotional experience is vital to music therapy for it enhances the responsiveness of the group and simultaneously fosters the personal development of each child within it.

Individual children are often drawn to different facets of musical-emotional experience, finding in the inherent qualities of certain songs something of an answer to their personal emotional needs.

The majority of children's songs can be described as "happy." Every bright, positive, cheery song falls into this category. These are songs that awaken, arouse from apathy or dullness, and stimulate response. They can be gently playful, or zestful and boisterous. The extent to which they can actually inspire happiness varies from song to song; some are emotionally weak, others really have an uplifting impact. Their therapeutic effect as bestowers of good spirits, alertness, and friendy cheerfulness needs no pointing out.

Example:

There are many purposeful songs in the literature. They ask a question or have something to get done, and often set actions to music. When their emotional character is forceful, with both melody and harmony adding drive, the children's involvement in the words and actions will be intensified. They give experiences of adventure, anticipation, humor, and the satisfaction of accomplishment. Much of the children's therapeutic engagement in the singing sessions and the growth of their participation develop in the focused activity these songs provide.

Example:

Bill's Train*

Go - ing to the sea, to the sea, to the sea, come home a - gain,
Go - ing to the sea, to the sea, to the sea, come home a - gain,

* A row of chairs is set out to make the "train". The "driver" is chosen, seated at the front and given the train whistle. (A three-tone train whistle is recommended.) He blows the whistle as indicated in the music. During the second verse the teacher chooses one or more children to sit in the train. They are given maracas, musical rattles, wooden clappers, etc., to shake in rhythm to the song. This verse can be repeated until the train is nearly full. Then the following verses are sung:

3rd Verse- **Just another seat on the train,** *etc.*
(the last children get on the train)
4th Verse- **Slowly up the hill on the train,** *etc.*
(this verse to be sung in a slow tempo)
5th Verse- **Quickly down the hill on the train,** *etc.*
(this verse to be sung in a very fast tempo)
6th Verse- **Going for a ride on the train,** *etc.*
(this is to be sung in the original tempo and is followed by the Coda)

Thoughtful songs appear less frequently in children's song books. And few of those that do are suitable for retarded children. This is a pity for such songs have much to give to this work. Their calm, slow melodies often appeal to children who are emotionally disturbed. For hyperactive children they provide a stability of experience that is lacking in the fast pulse of most cheery songs. Children who are deeply unhappy because of a painful home life or a difficult emotional pathology can experience, in thoughtful songs, a warmth of consolation and an immediacy of meaning that they cannot find in songs that express a gaiety they do not feel.

Example:

Something Is Going To Happen *

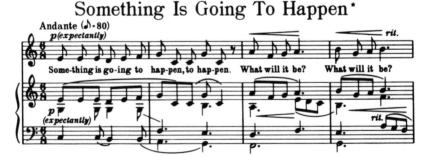

Some-thing is go-ing to hap-pen, to hap-pen. What will it be? What will it be?

* After singing the song through, the boys and the girls in the class can be seated together and the song repeated antiphonally, boys and girls alternating phrases. They should sing the last phrase together. It can then be sung again reversing the order of singing. The children will enjoy singing quietly and mysteriously.
© Copyright 1962 by Theodore Presser Co.   All Rights Reserved   International Copyright Secured
411 - 41011 - 19   Printed in U.S.A.

34

There are never enough lyric songs available for handicapped children. These songs have a direct, unalloyed emotional quality. A child singing a lyric song lives in feelings that are evoked and sustained by melody; children listening to a lyric song can share the same experiences. Most handicapped children have unformed feelings of tenderness, sweetness, reverence, and wonder, which life offers them little opportunity to realize and express. The beauty and gentleness of lyric songs can bring out these emotions and create a mood of delicacy and lightness around the group. Girls, particularly, find a great serenity in singing them.

Example:

Can You Sing To The Sun?

Gently (♩ = 48)

1. Can you sing to the sun? Can you whis-tle to the sun?
2. Can you sing to the moon? Can you whis-tle to the moon?
3. Can you sing to the stars? Can you whis-tle to the stars?

4. Can you sing to the cloud? *etc.*
5. Can you sing to the sky? *etc.*

The four broad groupings above describe most children's songs, yet there are others that bring special emotional experiences. Songs that combine the seriousness of the thoughtful song with the emotional quality of the lyric often express *sadness, tenderness,* or *longing.* Such intensities of feeling should be brought into singing sessions, else the children will be deprived of developmental emotional experience; life loses part of its deeper reality for them if sadness and longing remain unportrayed. Tenderness is especially important to impaired children.

Example:

Crying Song

This song was composed for a child who was crying. He had good reason to cry, but several children were mocking him. As we sang the song, their mood became less superficial and unkind. The song accepted the child's grief and then lifted the whole class into singing with pleasure. When we finished, the children were in a gentle mood, and the sad child was consoled.

This song lends itself well to antiphonal singing.

Words with a happy content can be elevated by a vivid lyrical melody into *joyousness* or into *triumph*. These dynamic experiences go beyond happiness and excitement to thrill the children. Expressed in singing, at the climax of a play or story, or after genuine achievement, true joy and deserved triumph are unforgettable.

Example:

Suggestions for Playing

The achievement of therapeutic goals in group singing is greatly helped when you are thoroughly familiar with the songs you are going to use. If you can memorize them, your playing will have freedom and flexibility; freedom from the score will make it possible for you to give your utmost attention to how the children, as a group and as individuals, are singing; flexibility will enable you to adjust tempo, dynamics, phrasing, etc., so that your playing will be appropriate to the musical situation at any moment.

Use your pianistic resources to enliven the familiar songs. The simple melodies, harmonies, and rhythms of most children's songs invite musical, expressive elaboration. Play the melody in octaves, make the harmony more interesting, vary repetitions; this will keep the song musically alive for the children (and for yourself).

Play with awareness and pleasure. Your positiveness will flow into your fingertips, be communicated to the children, and stimulate their awareness and pleasure.

Use a wide range of dynamics; all the gradations between very loud and very soft are vital means of expression and of reinforcing the children's musical experiences.

Pedal sparingly and with care. Do not hold the pedal down through melodic phrases; connect each tone with a new pedal if you wish or need to, but be sure each tone sounds distinctly. Pedal harmonies so that chords are also clean, with no tones from any chord sounding along with those of another.

If your pianistic abilities are limited, put an extra effort into your playing to give it vitality. The children will enjoy your effort and good will.

Listen to the children's singing; use a dynamic that enables you to hear them, for this will disclose what, in the song, they find easy and what they find difficult to sing. There may be places in many songs where most of them stop; note the places where they start again. Find out where the trouble lies. Be aware of the children who are not singing at all. Is there a song they will find irresistible? This kind of self-informing through listening can become a practical guide to your work.

Tempo

The tempo you use will make all the difference between an enthusiastic and an apathetic reception of a song. You may have to begin your work on a fast song below the proper tempo until the children know the words, understand them, and can enunciate them. They then will enjoy singing more quickly, and will make the extra effort required to sing the familiar words at the faster tempo. Conversely, you may have to introduce a slow song at a moderate tempo, and gradually play it slower after the children have learned the words and have grasped the musical shape of its melody. Then they will be ready to use the consciousness and control necessary for slow singing.

Be sensitive to the effect of tempo on a song; when it is correct, the melody and harmony can establish the intended mood. Regardless of how beautifully a song is written, if it is played in the wrong tempo the beneficial experience will be marred.

Tempos should be set with pianistic authority but they should rarely be mechanically rigid, beat by beat, throughout. Feel the expressive meaning of the words as they change from one phrase to the next. Let your tempos vary very slightly to vivify and emphasize these experiences, to free the singers from a metronomic beat and bring the song to life.

Vocal Range and Transposition

Many handicapped children have low-pitched voices; this vocal condition cannot be improved by using songs in keys too high for them. As a general rule, the C an octave above Middle C should be the upper limit. However, an occasional higher tone, so placed that there is time to take a breath before it is sung, can be a fine singing experience for children. For the lower limit, the B, A, even G below Middle C seldom present any difficulty. If the songs you wish to use are too high in pitch, transpose them to lower keys. Transposition is an essential part of playing for handicapped children's singing; write out your transpositions beforehand if you are unable to transpose freely at the moment.

Working with Vocally Limited Children

Many handicapped children can sing only two or three tones, usually quite low in pitch. When working in small groups these children can be singled out and called to the piano. If they are timid or insecure, careful individual attention will encourage them. Sing softly with each child the tones he can sing, while playing those tones, or chords containing them; then see if you can extend his range by introducing a tone higher and/or lower. For example:

Martha could sing only the B, A, G below Middle C. The pianist sang her name to these tones, making them into a slow descending phrase that was easy for her to sing.

Mar - tha   Jones

This phrase intrigued her and the pianist encouraged her to sing it with him. As they repeated it together, Martha became surer of the tones and sang with more strength. She was enjoying both the individual attention and singing her name, so the pianist developed the phrase to:

Mar - tha Jones can sing

After a few tries, she was able to sing this. In the next session she came to the piano with anticipation. The work of the previous session was repeated and when it was well established and she seemed confident, the pianist extended the phrase to:

Mar - tha Jones can sing a song.

The new tones, with their rhythmic variety and important words, stimulated her and immediately evoked an imitation. She seemed aware of what she had done, but was unable to repeat it. By going back to the simpler phrase, the pianist was able to rebuild her confidence and bring her to singing the extended phrase with intention. This was repeated the following week.

In each succeeding session the pianist spent a little time on Martha's singing, widening her range by selectively using songs she knew, often transposing them to suit her voice. After eleven sessions she was able to sing from the E below Middle C to the B above it. This made real singing possible for her in the group; she had a good memory for words and found considerable pleasure and fulfillment in the freedom singing gave her.

Transposition is of the greatest help in extending the vocal range of individual children. In addition to transposing complete songs, take any simple, familiar phrase the child can sing and raise or lower it a semi-tone or a tone as soon as you feel he is secure enough to try for the new tones. When working with individuals ask the others to join in singing from time to time. Almost always the children in the group become intensely interested in their classmate's "singing lesson" and in the progress he makes.

40

Accompanying the Child Singing Solo

Individual children who sing well should be asked to perform for the group. This will inspire others, who feel less able, to volunteer to sing a solo. Each child in turn should stand by the piano where you can see and work with him easily, and in such a position that he can also be seen and heard by the "audience." Play carefully for him, for this can be an important moment to him.

Your playing should be delicate for a child with a small voice. First let him hear the melody. Adjust the tempo to a speed comfortable for him, and, if necessary, transpose the song to suit his vocal range. You may have to sing softly with this child and wait for him to repeat each tone after you. Encourage him by leaning a little toward him, letting him feel your attention. Use little or no pedal; let each chord clear before playing the next, but bring out each tone of the melody with your finger so that its outline is clear to him. The dynamics you use should always suit the volume of tone each child is able to bring forth.

For a child whose voice flies off pitch because of nervousness or inattention, it is usually enough to ask him gently to listen, and then play the phrase for him.

If a child sings much too fast, let him go through the song once in his tempo, and then repeat it more slowly for him to hear. It may help if you take one of his hands and move it in the correct tempo while playing the melody with your other hand.

You may be able to increase the tonal volume of the child whose voice is almost inaudible by having him stand in a good singing position: relaxed, looking straight ahead, one hand lying in the palm of the other at waist level, legs slightly apart.

When songs are used in which the "soloist" sings antiphonally with the other children, their attention is kept upon him and his effort while their responsiveness adds to his pleasure and bolsters his courage.

Solo singing is a many-sided experience for the children who do it and for those who listen; each child's personality stands out in his singing.

Bringing Children to the Piano

Many children will want to come to you at the piano; most will want to play it. Part of the singing session can be devoted to taking each child in turn and, with his index finger, playing the melody of a song he has chosen. This is one way of bringing children closer to the music and to you. It can be an intimate activity and an incentive to warmer participation.

There are endless opportunities for therapeutic happenings to individuals in group-singing in addition to the more general gains in awareness, achievement, social feeling, etc., that it can produce. Consistent work in this area leads to the realization that each element and component of music possesses a therapeutic potential of its own.

In groups of singing children there will be individuals who are benefiting, in their particular way, from the effects that these elements and components have upon them. In singing, making a *ritard,* an *accelerando,* making a *diminuendo* and a *crescendo* can bring to bear, on some particular child, a specific therapeutic influence. One child can be developing himself as he acquires the alertness needed to sing antiphonal phrases; another, who is perhaps apathetic, can wake up to the active situation with the children around him as he sings songs with dissonant harmonies.

The growth of personality of each individual within the group will raise the responsive level of that group to everyone's benefit. When children experience music so consciously and personally that it works developmentally upon them, they take their music activities ever more seriously. They put more of their essential selves into their singing, and song becomes a vital part of life for them.

Leading the Singing Group

Forty to fifty children are generally the largest numbers one would consider practical for regular assemblies. Whenever possible avoid mixing older children with young children new to

42

school life, especially when the older ones have had so much singing experience that they need to work on a more advanced level. For either the older ones will be held back, or the younger ones denied their proper introduction to singing. However, if you work with comparatively small groups of around twenty, it is quite possible to take children of mixed ages and work flexibly with the abilities and needs of individuals within the group. The most productve work with handicapped children can be done when the groups do not exceed 12 in number. Sessions can be from 20 to 60 minutes in length, depending on the children and on the materials used.

Know thoroughly the songs you are going to use. You will then be free to concentrate on the best way to direct the children and work with their responses.

It is important to have a variety of songs to present. Introduce new songs by singing them to the children. Ask them to listen before they attempt to sing. If the song is simple, after several repetitions of verse or action, encourage them to join in as they get the idea. Difficult words and more complex phrases may be taught by having the group or individual children speak them after you, but do this as little as possible; try to introduce every song in such a way that the children experience words, music, idea, and mood as a unity from the beginning.

When the children are familiar with a few songs, separate the boys and girls into two groups. Have the boys listen to the girls sing and vice-versa. This should not be done competitively. Select suitable songs in which successive phrases can be sung by boys and girls antiphonally. This is a good way of bringing more consciousness and expression into children's singing.

Example:

A Rainy Day

GIRLS   BOYS   GIRLS

do____ on a rain-y day?__ We'll go to sleep__ on a rain-y

The entire song can be repeated as many times as the teacher and the class may wish with the variations supplied by the child's or children's answers to the teacher's question, "What else would you like to do today?" One child might say, for example, "Let's go outside." That child then stands and sings "Let's go outside on a rainy day," from the repeat sign. All the children then join in the second phrase ("That's what we'll do on a rainy day.").

The description of the weather can be varied to suit the day: cloudy, windy, snowy, foggy.

The words, mood and tempo of the song should be freely adapted to the children's suggestion's ("lazily", "lively", "happily", "brightly", "sadly", are all possibilities). The tempo could be as fast as ♩. = 96.

The two given alternate notes in the melody should not be sung unless absolutely necessary.

Antiphonal singing is effective with a variety of songs. Conduct the groups carefully. If the song is slow and lyrical, the children can gain a melodic experience from listening to each other. If it is quick and tricky, they will have to be alert to your directing and exercise control to sing the right phrases at the right time.

In everything you do in singing classes, in directing unison, antiphonal, or individual singing, let your leadership be clear and purposeful. Realize that each song offers a particular scope of experience and direct the singing of it so that all it has to give may become an active reality for the children.

Although you will have definite objectives in mind for every session and for the songs you plan to use, be prepared to change your program if some unexpected, promising responses come from the children. Take these up and work to utilize them. Handicapped children's developing responsiveness is easily overwhelmed, their tentative impulses to express something of their inner experiences are all too easily thwarted. Overinsistence upon adhering to a planned program can mean missing an important message from the children and losing an opportunity for creative, therapeutic work.

Be delicate in working with newly manifesting responses from timid, young, or withdrawn children; it is often better to use a careful, indirect approach with them. Give them the opportunity to enjoy themselves in their growing freedom and deepening participation before, for example, calling on any one of them to sing alone before the group. A feeling for timing is necessary here. One child may need many weeks before participating so directly. Another, stimulated by his experiences and confident in the situation, will be ready to sing to the group after only three or four sessions; in so doing he may disclose an unsuspected musical sensitivity.

When an individual child sings solo before the group, support rather than lead. As often as possible step aside—or sit down—and allow him to feel and realize his own initiative and to be the focus of everyone's attention. Be encouraging to every child during his turn—whether his voice may be weak, his speech underdeveloped, or his capacity to carry a tune limited. In using singing as therapy, participation is much more important than performance, particularly with the young or more severely handicapped. Insist that all the children listen to such a child. If the song he sings contains phrases which the whole group can sing after him, or in answer to him, lead the group while the pianist supports the child.

The group will usually want to applaud the singer but unfortunately the clapping, cheering, and laughter of handicapped children are frequently mimicry of television audiences, and not genuine expressions of appreciation; their pleasure is in the activity of applauding and not in what should have occasioned it. If this kind of applause is allowed to persist in your singing sessions, a mood of carelessness and indiscrimination is encouraged that will intrude upon the working spirit you are trying to build. Help the children to learn that applause is a meaningful expression of recognized accomplishment. Then it will have value for everyone.

Conduct stimulating songs with vitality but proportion the amount of energy you use to the size of the group. Your hand movements should define the melodic rhythm of the song rather than merely beat time.[1]

Sing with warmth and pleasure as you lead. Form the words clearly with decisive movements of your mouth and tongue to help the children with their enunciation. Especially emphasize the first and final consonants, but do not overexaggerate your facial movements to the point where they become strange to the children. If your singing voice is weak, your conviction will carry it; if it is strong, be careful not to let it take over and dominate the singing. A full voice, with a rich tonal quality,

[1]Signing with singing is not discussed in this text. See *Music for the Hearing Impaired—and Other Special Groups*, page 82.

should be used with care and discrimination. Do not sing as you would in public, and never let your voice's melodic power obscure the words. Keep your singing child-oriented, true to the experiences of children singing their songs.

Bearing in mind the handicaps of the children in your group, work to make their singing as musical as possible. Break up any grossly mechanical or habitual responses to music such as rhythmically overemphasized, unthinking singing, or ebullient, abandoned yelling of songs. First, work for the more fundamental musical experiences in a variety of songs that give a wide range of tempo, dynamics, and mood. Lead the children into the fun of making changes in dynamics and tempo; conduct ritards on the ending phrases.

Older children who have made progress in singing, or those whose vocal abilities are less heavily impaired by pathology, are ready for some musical challenge. Work on the vocal quality of their singing, on good vowel sounds, on the holding of tones, on phrasing and expression. Musically gifted handicapped children need the special nourishment that expressively directed singing can give them. Their predisposition to music, related as it is to both their emotional life and intelligence, is integral to their personalities.

Believe in everything you do with and for the children. Place yourself and your abilities at the service of their needs and experiences. The dullness of repetitive routine should never be allowed to settle into the sessions. Always work progressively for the next step in the development of as many children in the group as you can. Maintain the quality and the content of the sessions consistently from week to week; each session will be the firm rung of a ladder of progress which the children may mount.

Chapter Two

Resonator Bells

A set of resonator bells is a versatile instrument for leading handicapped children into engaging, structured group activity. The bells are physically uncomplicated and sturdy to handle; clear tones result from the straightforward, direct action of striking. They can be used selectively, with just those bells required for any one piece of musical work being given separately to children so as to simplify and organize their playing.

Resonator bells gain their significance in group activities from the music with which they are used and from the way their tones are integrated into it. In selected musical contexts they give distinct experiences of pitch, tonal relationships and qualities of intervals, the rise and fall of tones in melodies, the placement of tones in both chordal harmonies and melodically formed harmonies, and the root tones of chords. By arranging certain bells to emphasize—in well-defined rhythmic organization— salient melodic-harmonic components in a composition or song, activity-experiences can be created which children will find meaningful and attractive. The simplest arrangements, in which each bell is prominent and telling, are often the most effective.

Any number of children may participate in such arrangements, although with handicapped children, progressive work results most directly when two, three, or four children each play single, or small groups of bells. Arrangements may also be made in which the parts vary in complexity and so will be appropriate for various levels of ability.

An attractive variety of bell arrangements may be made with songs the children know. Such songs provide a familiar stepping-off point for instrumental work while becoming more interesting and enjoyable to the children through the special tonal experiences—rhythmic, melodic, and harmonic—the bells create in them. A secure basis for therapeutic work is thus established.

When a child's part in an arrangement has a definite role and is musically effective, he will become increasingly involved in playing it. Through his attentiveness to his part and to its interrelationship with the parts of the children with whom he is playing, he perceives and remembers the overall musical experience. His awareness grows. His cooperation with the musician and/or teacher who leads him and the musical success this achieves stabilize his participation in the work of the group.

The experiences a child gets with resonator bells can lead him into using his ability to listen, and into developing conscious tonal-melodic receptiveness. He may develop pitch discrimination and eventually improve his singing capacity. Should the child lack physical coordination or control, its development will be stimulated as he works to sound the tones of the bells he plays in their musically designated places. He can become more musically responsive, and so gain substantial fulfillment from all his musical experiences and activities.

Resonator bells are effective with children of all ages, but their tone quality and construction make them particularly suitable for younger ones. When used with the youngest children in the school as the first tonal instrument they play, resonator bells give a musically varied and well-formed introduction to group instrumental activities.

A Special Way of Introducing Resonator Bells

An effective introduction to resonator bells, particularly for young children, can be made by choosing a short rhythmic song containing contrasting melodic phrases in question-and-answer form. Arrange the song for two children, each to play one bell— one child playing during the question phrases, the other during the answer ones. The tone of each bell must sound well with the melody and harmony of the phrases in which it plays. Often the

48

tonic and dominant tones of the key of the song will be ideally suitable.

Example:

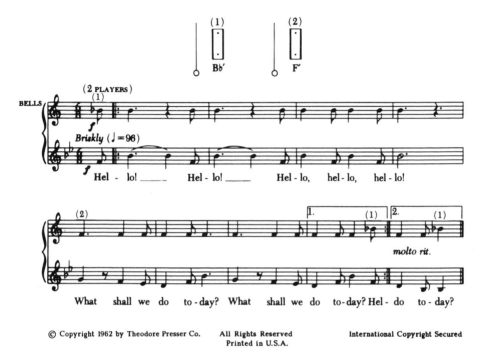

Set out the F and B♭ bells on a table before the class and have children come up two at a time to play them, or arrange the class in a three-quarter circle and move the bells around the group on a low table (see photographs). Play and sing the song in a moderate tempo. Direct each child to play his bell during the phrases allotted to it, but leave him free to play his own response to the song's rhythmic structure and tempo. As the children take turns, each one's playing will reveal much about the state of development of his musical responsiveness. This information will be relevant to the planning of immediate and future work with the group.

The following kinds of responses are representative of average groups of mentally retarded, emotionally disturbed, brain-injured, or physically handicapped children.

Introducing resonator bells with the "Hello" song; the piano bench with the bells on it will be moved around the group. Some children are relatively advanced—for them, two bells to be played together are given to the first part to increase its challenge. The players concentrate, and are the focus of everyone's attention and pleasure.

The bells have moved around, the children on the right have had their turn, those on the left await theirs; the mutual interest is good. An emotionally disturbed boy beats in an inflexible tempo unrelated to the music; the girl watches the pianist closely, poised to play on the first note of her phrase.

Children One and Two

The first child's beating is sporadic and has no rhythmic relationship to the song; he strikes the bells any number of times in short, irregular impulses. Child two beats the basic beat.

Children Three and Four

Child three plays on the emphasized beats of the melody—or on the stressed syllables in the verbal setting. Child four beats duplets regardless of the triplet character of the song's rhythmic structure.

Children Five and Six

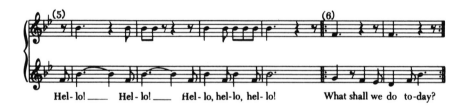

The fifth child is sensitive to the melodic structure and is attempting to beat its rhythm. Child six plays the first beat of every measure.

Children Seven and Eight

Child seven beats a continuous beat in a constant tempo that is unrelated to the tempo of the song. The eighth child plays the melodic rhythm of his phrase.

Children Nine and Ten

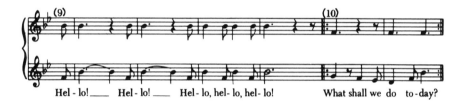

The melodic rhythm is played by child nine; the basic beat, with occasional beats missed, by child ten.

Children eight and nine show a sensitivity to the melody of the song and/or a clear grasp of the rhythm in which its words are sung. They also demonstrate physical control and the ability to participate in resonator bell work with some degree of perceptive alertness. Child five is approaching this level of ability.

Children two, three, six, and ten are less musically awake but their responses show rhythmic feeling and are free from rhythmic disturbance. The playing of children one, four, and seven manifests rhythmic disturbance; there is confusion—child four—and the lack of any functioning, integrated rhythmic sense —children one and seven. Each child's response indicates directly an immediate goal for work with him.

The children who can, or who are attempting to play the melodic rhythm should have the opportunity of playing together to experience the clearly defined question-and-answer interplay between their parts and between the tonic and dominant tones they sound. As they repeat the activity in succeeding sessions they will be able to master this rhythmic form fully and absorb the experience, at the same time demonstrating it in its completeness to the other members of the group. They should take turns at playing both parts. Variations of the experience may be introduced when appropriate to the players and to the group by playing and singing the song with different dynamics and with changes of tempo.

Children two, three, six, and ten should repeat the activity consistently, each child having turns at both parts of the arrangement, and playing with different children. The aim here is to lead these children into playing the melodic rhythm. In this arrangement the playing of the melodic rhythm yields the most explicit musical activity-experience, one that can result only from a musically functioning unity of sustained awareness and both physical and emotional control. Many handicapped children show a deficiency in perception, or in physical control due to injury or underdeveloped coordination, or in emotional stability, as expressed in scattered behavior and the inability to sustain responsive activity. When a child whose condition includes some measure of these handicaps becomes caught up in the experience of the melodic form and works directedly to play its rhythm, he is beginning to overcome his impairment. His playing is integrating newly developing capacities for listening, remembering, concentration, and physical control into a responsive capability.

The tendency to progress in this direction develops as the children become more familiar and involved with the arrangement through participating in it, and, if not yet capable, through hearing and seeing the melodic rhythm played by those who can do it. The pianist may also help by playing only the melodic rhythm of the song; all other notes that are "outside" the melodic rhythm, such as parts of the accompaniment, are omitted. Emphasize the melodic rhythm still further by not sustaining tones; in this case the rhythmic structures of the phrases are stressed by not holding any tone longer than a quarter note, or even an eighth note.

With those children who show rhythmic disturbances, aim to bring them into experiencing the song musically and meaningfully so that their playing begins to express this experience and becomes free from rhythmic disorder. A first step toward this is to change your playing of the song to fit it rhythmically to each child's playing. Then his limited use of his bell has the possibility of acquiring musical significance for him.

For example, as child four begins to play, quickly change the meter of the phrase to 4/8, thus ordering his beating as follows:

Return to 6/8 time for child three's playing.

For child seven, play and sing the song in his tempo, thus making his playing the basic beat. Or if his playing is fast, treat it as duplets and play the phrases in which he beats in 4/8, as above. If his beating is very fast, consider each beat an eighth note and play the song in 6/8 in the tempo his playing sets. Play the song as written for child eight.

As these children become aware of and establish some relationship between their playing and the song, begin to lead their playing toward the song's normal tempo. It is possible that as they develop some degree of musical perception of the song they will begin spontaneously to play in its correct tempo.

Such changes of tempo and meter as these stimulate the musical attentiveness of the children, particularly in those for whom the changes are made. It may be a help when working with such a child to have a more musically able child as his playing partner.

With child one, it can be hoped that repeated experiences of other children's playing may sensitize him and lead him into discovering significance in playing some part of the song's melodic-rhythmic structure. However, more direct and effective work may be done by giving him some *individual* tonal-rhythmic attention. Play freely in a key that suits the tone of his bell and imitate his playing rhythmically to make him more conscious of it, or to set up a give-and-take response with him. This technique can bring directedness and possibly some order into his playing. By improvising simple music around his playing you may then be able to engage him on some level of musical response. At any suitable time, when the child's attention has been musically drawn to his use of the bell, reintroduce the song.

Pervading all the introductory work that can be done in this arrangement is the experience of the interrelationship of the tonic and dominant tones in the song's melodic-harmonic structure. This underlies each child's experience, whether he is playing a bell or watching others play. Even if those who play have little or no rhythmic awareness, the sounding of these two tones in alternating sections of the song gives their activity a tonal organization. When the players are musically perceptive and play the melodic rhythm, this fundamental experience of tonal relationship and polarity is emphasized for the entire group.

Making Resonator Bell Arrangements

An ongoing resonator bell program can lead children into a range of activities and experiences through a series of varied musical arrangements in which they each play definite parts. For this purpose songs are chosen with a diversity of mood, tempo, key, content, rhythmic structure, etc., the bell parts graded in complexity from simple to relatively advanced. The way the parts are set into a song will determine the quality and extent of the children's participation, and thus what they will gain from playing them.

When making an arrangement a teacher is concerned directly with the character and quality of the experiences she is creating for children, through which she will work to involve them. Within the overall experience of the arrangement each bell part is going to create its special effect. This will be experienced in different ways: *directly* by the child who plays it; *in relation to their own parts* by children who also play in the arrangement; *as an integral feature of the total arrangement* by those in the group who are watching and hearing. In this way each characteristic a bell part possesses becomes an essential attribute of a total experience which can arouse and focus the children's interest, and draw them into mutually responsive activity, giving them satisfaction and pleasure. The more the various parts' *forms of activity* are perceivably and mentally comprehensible, and the sharper the definition of *the musical effects* they create, the more effective will the arrangement be as a vehicle for music therapy.

To these two basic requirements—a distinctly formed activity and a telling musical effect—is to be added a third, that all the parts in an arrangement should possess an interesting interrelationship. They should be so designed that their interplay makes "attractive sense" to children, even to having a musical game-like quality. Such parts can be similar—the form of one child's playing being duplicated by another; or contrasting—one part being set off by the different form of another.

The ten examples that follow have been selected to show that resonator bells are most effectively used when the parts they play have defined musical identity in the context of each song. This is facilitated by arranging the bell parts to play definite musical components which are expressively appropriate to the song and enhance its experience. Among the components played by bells in the illustrations are: intervals, scale forms, rhythmic patterns, principal melodic tones, countermelodies, melodic phrase structures, question-and-answer phrases, canon forms, consonant and dissonant harmonies, rhythmic punctuation, accent, and contrast. The way these are used in the various songs is determined by each song's content and quality, by the opportunities its structure offers for arrangement, and by considerations of what would be most meaningful to the children who play in it.

The foregoing characteristics are discussed in detail with the examples, and for each one an attempt is made to elucidate the experiential value the arrangement and its parts hold for the players.

When reading the examples, visualize a classroom situation in which the bells for any particular arrangement are set out on a table in keyboard order for the players. (This is described more fully in Directing Resonator Bell Work.) The players face the group and are easily seen by them and the pianist. Children take turns at playing parts. In the text, each part is numbered in the order of its appearance in the arrangement.

1. Each tone of a melody may be played by the bells, various phrases being played by different children. The interest of the arrangement is increased when the form of the song's melody gives contrasting experiences to the players.

Example:

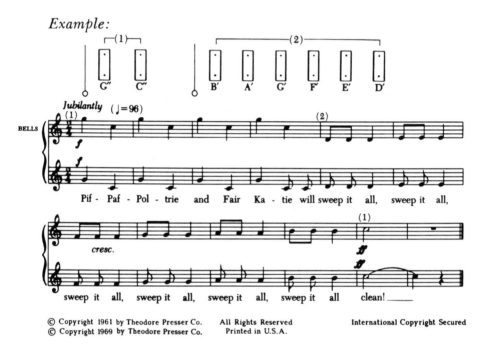

The entire melody is played on the bells with the exception of one tone. (This may be played spontaneously by some children but is not specified in the arrangement.) Each part is well defined and has an immediate musical purpose: Child one plays alternately on the basic beat the tones of the 5th interval—and so creates a fundamental experience in scale and chord structures; child two plays six of the seven scale tones in ascending sequence, to a repeating simple rhythmic pattern. The clarity of such parts as these, the distinct difference between them, and the complete musical effect their combination creates increase an

58

arrangement's capacity for engagement. The children's pleasure in it leads them into concentrating on their parts; they enjoy the feeling of musical purposefulness in the activity, and the musical success which results.

The interest of children whose abilities are less developed is stimulated by their watching, listening, and/or singing as others play, and by the musical and physical characteristics of such parts. They become eager to play the bells and may make impressive efforts to master them when they are given their turn.

The interrelationship of the two parts also carries an active social effect: child one begins with the repeating affirmative tonal statement; the lead then passes to child two; his playing builds toward the climax as his rhythmic pattern ascends the scale, but the completing tone of the scale—the climax—must be played by child one. The awareness and sense of mutual participation this develops helps to generate readiness for group work.

2. The melodic experience of a lyric song may be intensified by a bell arrangement. This is done most effectively when the bell tones do not double every note of the melody but emphasize its rise and fall by accenting the important and expressive tones.

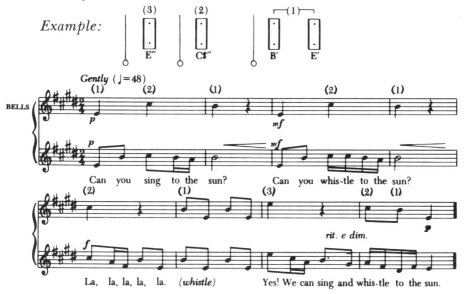

As the children play they create a lyric-melodic experience. The mood of their participation takes on this calmly emotional quality and becomes an expression of the feeling content of the song—a contrast to the melodic/rhythmic concentration and activity of the previous example.

The internal structure of the arrangement gives the inter-activity of the players a feeling of melodic-expressive coordination. Children one and two work together in the first phrase and its repetition. Child two goes on to play the first note of the "la" singing. Child one then creates a rhythmic contrast by playing the alternating tones of the 5th interval, which support the whistling. His playing leads directly to the melodic peak of the song. This is played by child three—it is the only tone he plays in the arrangement and its importance to him is emphasized by this. He plays the note on which the questions in the song are answered by "Yes!"—the single high tone that completes the form of the melody; if he had other tones to play, they could only be anticlimactic and detract from its significance. In the last measure children one and two play in the harmonies of the cadence.

The children also experience the lyricism of the song, playing in its gentle tempo on the main beats of phrases, holding long rests between bell tones, and being aware of the emphasizing of important words in the setting.

3. Bell parts may enhance a melody by emphasizing its phrase forms.

Example:

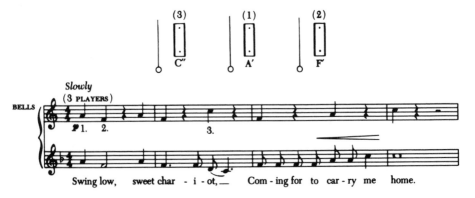

Swing low, sweet char - i - ot,___ Com- ing for to car - ry me home. I

As the three tones of the tonic triad play in unison with the melody, following its rise and fall, they bring out and sustain its lyric quality. In the second melodic phrase, two of the three tones sound a brief but effective countermelody. At the same time, each bell sounds a tone of the changing harmonies, further deepening the mood of the song. When the bells play together on the final chord and sound in consonance the tones that have been heard singly and as intervals, a beautiful musical effect is created. This is the first illustration in which bells play a chord; this experience is especially significant because it is used so sparingly, and at an appropriate and telling moment.

4. Arrangements may be made that call for alertness and quick striking of the bells. The musical experience of the 2nd interval is stressed in this example; in this song it is descriptively exciting.

Example:

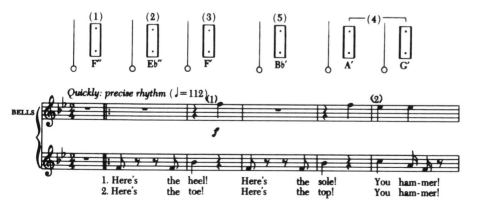

1. Here's   the heel!   Here's   the sole!   You ham-mer!
2. Here's   the toe!   Here's   the top!   You ham-mer!

61

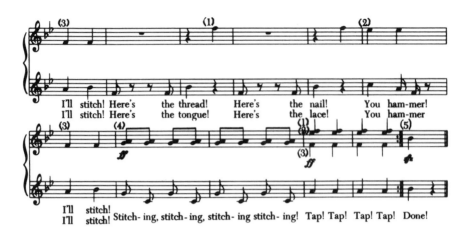

The usual keyboard order of setting out the bells is changed to suit the arrangement of the various parts. This makes it easier to conduct players one, two, and three when they play together and also gives them a feeling of ensemble. Additionally, this layout *stages* the bell-playing to give the children who are watching a clearly defined experience. In the last five measures, the climax begins on the right as child four repeats his quick dissonant duplets; the playing swings over to the left as the three children repeat the dominant 7th interval, and then moves to the child standing between these two groups of bells who resolves the preceding harmony with a single tone.

The most prominent experiences in this arrangement are the dissonances, and the activities of child four, who plays two bells simultaneously at a skill-demanding speed, and of child five, who ends the song with the single tone he plays. There is an extra musical challenge to this part: the cadence which leads to it is repeated twice, but the first time it is resolved directly by the repetition of the melody. Child five must hold his note back until the end of the second repetition. His position between the players of the two chords which his tone resolves adds to the stimulation of his experience.

5. The emphasizing of any specific interval gives a particular character to an arrangement, as does the octave in the following example.

Example:

The first three parts follow the melodic outline of the song in ascending octaves, which carry a feeling of affirmation. The dissonance in the fourth measure, played during the accompanist's rest on the third beat, is a stimulating, arousing harmonic pre-

63

paration for singing the birthday child's name. The ascending octaves are repeated, bringing their quality of brightness and gaiety to the word "birthday." The single bell played when soloist and group sing antiphonally provides musical support and contrast.

Bells can increase the ceremonial importance of a song, in this case adding to the pleasure and excitement of birthday celebrations.

6. Arrangements can be made in which the children play entirely on the rests.

Example:

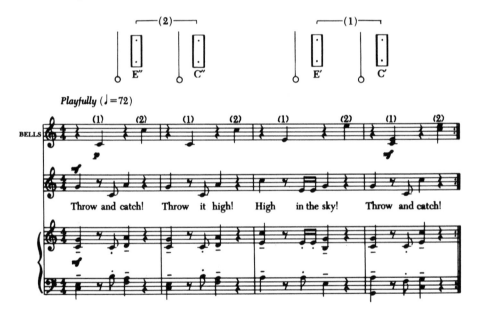

Each tone the players sound stands out distinctly in a rest and provides a rhythmic-tonal emphasis of the melody. Child one always plays on the second beat in the measure, child two on the fourth; together, they alternate with the piano in sustaining the basic beat. Their parts are rhythmically identical and the interest and charm of the piece results from the alternation of low and high as child two repeats, an octave higher, the tone child one has played. The interval experiences that give this arrangement its characteristic sound are those of the octave and the major third.

7. Bell parts may echo, answer, or imitate a melodic phrase in the manner of a canon.

Example:

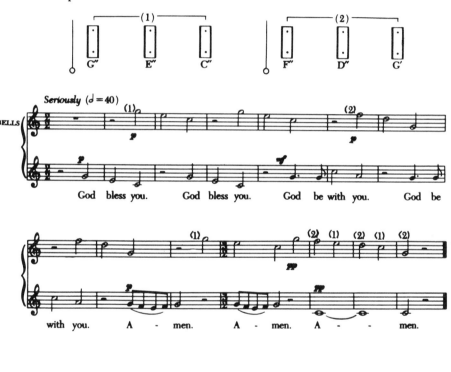

The singers and the players are presented with an experience of canonlike melodic harmonization, a rich tonal experience that can develop musical attentiveness. Very few of these children

65

are able to gain such an experience through singing, but they may receive it here through bell tones.

The serious mood of the song is enhanced by the bell parts; their order and musical meaning give the arrangement a calm, stable effect. Notice that the players' alternation of complete phrases changes at the end of the song to a closer interaction of music-making in the alternating of each note of the phrases in succession. This kind of contrast of activity and tonal experience adds interest and character to an arrangement.

8. Bells can answer the phrases of a melody with contrasting phrases. These may be repeated on different scale tones and in different time values.

Example:

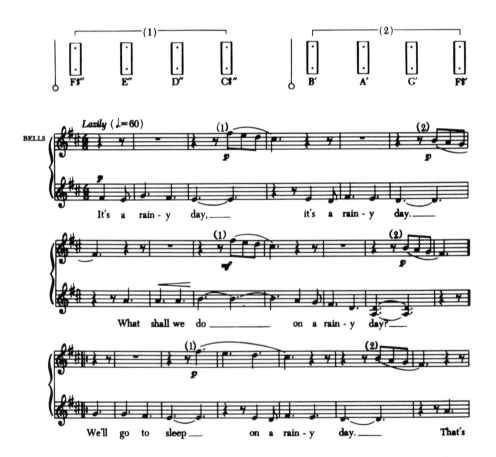

what we'll do _____ on a rain - y day. __

Through the harmonic structure of the song, the two phrases played by the bells—which are identical in tonal structure—acquire a question-and-answer relationship, with the musical question sounded by child one's phrase being answered by child two's. As they sound antiphonally, beginning each time over the last tone of a song-phrase, they make an attractive alternation of related, yet contrasting, tonal experience. When, in the second part of the song, phrase one is augmented—its former eighth notes now dotted quarter notes—the experience of its tonal line is emphasized, as is the tempo of the song phrase which it imitates. That the following repetition of phrase two remains in its original form keeps the arrangement rhythmically alive and gives the succeeding playing of phrase one—again in dotted quarters—a stronger expressive character. As the last repetition of phrase two, now also in augmentation, continues the line, the complete descending scale-form makes an interesting countermelody to the song's concluding phrase. Such an arrangement can yield a strong experience of the interdependence of parts.

Note also, in this example, that the answering phrase does not end on the tonic but on the third note of the scale, thereby retaining a feeling of suspension in keeping with the mood of the song.

The techniques of augmentation and diminution, in which the time values of notes are made respectively longer and shorter, bring variety into the forms of the players' activities, and create experiences which promote a deeper awareness of melodic phrase and a feeling for the significance of tempo.

9. For groups of educable children who have developed some proficiency in playing resonator bells, challenging and exciting arrangements can be made on an advanced, formal level. These need not be restricted to songs; instrumental music, carefully chosen, lends itself well to bell tones. Bach's *Anna Magdalena Book*, Schuman's *Children Scenes*, many of the Mozart minuets, etc., hold great possibilities for arrangements which will interest children, draw them into alert participation, and give them a sense of musical mastery.

Example:

Other sources of music for arrangements lie in selected folk, popular, patriotic, religious, and seasonal music, and in show tunes. The repertoire of choral music also holds possibilities; alto or tenor parts may be played by bells.

10. Bells may play effective and integral parts in especially composed group vocal works. This illustration is of a setting of the Twenty-third Psalm for speakers, singers, a resonator bell part for one player, and piano. The work was written for a class of teen-age educable girls.

The musical form of the work is ABCA. The Psalm begins with a phrase played by the bells without accompaniment. This establishes the tempo and a quiet, serious mood. The phrase is then repeated in unison and antiphonally with the singers. It has the character of an ostinato against the changing music of the piano part and is essential to the structure of this first section of the composition.

Example:

In the B section a repeated bell tone emphasizes the relationship of the changing harmonies played by the piano.

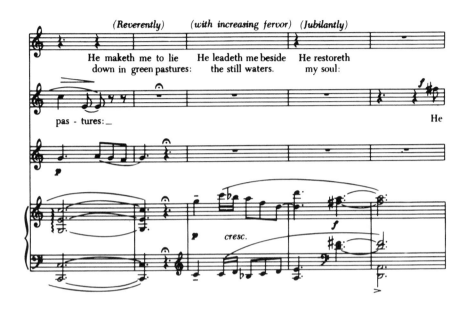

71

The C section begins with a change of key introduced by a motif of two tones played by the bells, unaccompanied, on the basic beats. This is then taken up by the singers and the piano.

In the final part of the work, the second A section repeats the bell phrase that was used in the opening, and the two-tone motif from the C section.

Throughout the entire composition the bells are melodically, harmonically, rhythmically, expressively, and structurally essential. The player who masters this part acquires extensive musical experience. He realizes the importance of the music he plays in the total work, and that he, alone, carries a large measure of responsibility for sustaining the quality of its performance. This is a challenge which, successfully met, gives the player a morale-building sense of achievement and pride.

See also *A Garden of Bell Flowers*. This collection illustrates many imaginative and musically effective ways of writing or arranging for resonator bells.

* * *

The foregoing principles of arrangement apply widely to the use of other single-toned pitched instruments, such as handbells and reed horns.

Experiences of Tone and Structure

There are two essential, entirely musical experiences fundamental to therapeutic work with resonator bells. The first concerns *tone*: there is for the bell player a penetrating quality to
the tone he creates with his bell. The action of striking his bell
relates him directly to the sound it makes. This tone—experienced as belonging intimately in pitch, harmony, and tonal
quality, to the sounds of the music he is hearing—acquires vivid,
sensory forcefulness. The sensation is sweet and pleasurable and
carries a clarity of musical experience that originates in the
tonal structure and expressive character of the arrangement.
Such sensations awaken a responsive center of specially developed musical sensitivity that can be activated in succeeding sessions to increase the child's participation in all their perceptual
and social aspects.

The second essentially musical experience concerns *structure*: through his participating activity, a child can become
closely aware of, and responsive to, the structure of an arrangement. His attentiveness as he waits to play, his experiences of
others playing, and of the order and musical placement of their
playing, draw him more consciously into the structure of the
arrangement's phrases. His own activity becomes identified with
the particular melodic passages in which he plays. In some arrangements he experiences his bell's tone in relation to the
harmonic-melodic structures that precede, accompany, and follow it; the flow of these musically ordered sequences of experience
engages his responding awareness. The tempo—the rhythmic
pulse in which the music "happens"—supports his part in it.
All this yields a sense of security, of being enclosed within a
total, meaningful structure. The sensations of tonal vividness
compound the significance of these experiences.

At some level the organization of the arrangement—to
him a composite of musical experience and of coactivity within
it—is impressed into the child's memory. This musical organization becomes to some extent an organization of self; the order of
it becomes part of his order, the expression of the music an
aspect of his feeling, and the purpose, the directedness of his

participation, something of a capacity for purposeful response.

These responses vary according to the individual. All manner of organic or psychological factors may intervene in a child's potential response and may limit his capacity to realize and sustain such experiences. Nevertheless, resonator bell activities hold the possibility for their development, and the majority of handicapped children do respond progressively and with commitment to the tonal-melodic sensations and musical structure in their bell work.

The Tonal Requirements of Resonator Bells

From the foregoing it can be seen that the tonal characteristics of the resonator bells being used directly affect the quality of the experiences they create. The effectiveness of music-making with them is most strongly realized when their tones are clear, full and dulcet, and possess good volume. They should be brilliant so as to sound strongly with piano and voices but should not persist too long to cause intrusive blurrings of tone or unintended dissonances when consecutive scale tones are played in a moderate tempo. No metallic percussive sound made by the beater striking the bar should be audible.

Many of the sets of bells currently available fulfill these specifications, some do not. Problematically, a number of the older sets in use in schools produce only thin, percussive sounds which lack tonal warmth. This can be due to the hardening of the beaters with age; such brittleness of tone may be remedied, often to a surprising extent, by using new, softer beaters, which can be purchased separately.

Some of the more recent designs, which use a plastic resonator chamber, are light in weight. They tend to bounce and rattle when used on a table if struck with the force needed to produce a big tone. If these bells are placed on foam-backed table mats or even on folded facial tissues, this is avoided and their excellent tonal characteristics are unmarred.

The tonal range of the standard set of bells, C' to G" affords scope for creating a great many musical experiences. Wider possibilities for pitch and tonal contrast can be obtained by using an extended set—G to G"—or by adding the extra tones G to B to a standard set.

Playing for Resonator Bell Work

It is essential that the piano be in tune with the bells. This may mean a special direction to the piano tuner when an old school piano is used.

Most of the directions given for pianists in the chapters on Singing and Instrumental Activities can be applied to playing arrangements or compositions for resonator bells. Sensitive, careful use of dynamics and pedaling will ensure the tonal effectiveness of the work.

Directing Resonator Bell Work

The bells required for an arrangement should be placed on a table of suitable height for standing players to strike them— in regular bell work it is usually preferable to have the children stand while playing. If for reasons of disability, class control, or any special purposes, the players are seated, the height of the table should be as little above the children's knees as possible.

Set out the bells, grouped into the respective parts, *in keyboard order for the players*. This is done specifically to accustom each child from the beginning to the low-left/high-right, standard layout of tones. In most of the illustrated arrangements, all the bells used are in this order; in others, the particular character of the arrangements require special groupings of bells. Here, however, the general layout keeps the highest tones to the players' right, and each child's group of bells is placed in keyboard order for him.

It will take but a little practical experience for you to become accustomed to working with the low and high tones reversed from their usual positions, particularly if you familiarize yourself with each arrangement beforehand by playing its parts on the bells set out as they will face you when you direct.

Insofar as possible, directing should be done from memory; repeated reference to a score while working will disconnect you from the children's response. A reminder of the structure of the arrangement may well be necessary immediately before beginning work with it. This can be made by writing out above the words of the song the notes of the bells where they play. Another time-saving device when selecting bells and setting them out, or when changing from one arrangement to another, is the kind of figurative sketch given here with each illustration. These indicate clearly the bells to be used, their layout as seen from the leader's position, and the number of beaters required. You will also direct with more assurance if you do not have to identify the tones of the various bells by the letters imprinted on the bars— these are often difficult to see. If needed, you can write the notes in large letters on the ends of the resonators, but this should be used as a supplementary aid only. If you can know when and in which order the various tones are played *by their positions in the bell layout* (this is how the children will learn and remember the arrangement), your conducting will be confident and your closeness to the children's work at its ultimate.

Sit on a low chair or kneel before the players when directing to make it easier for them to give their attention to you and their bells at the same time. Use small, clearly indicating hand movements to direct playing. Many children will require guidance with the physical action of playing. Some will not at first lift the beater from the bell when they have struck it; they must experience that this is necessary. A child with visual defects or lack of eye-hand coordination may have difficulty in hitting a bell positioned in the usual way with a narrow end toward him; he will probably do much better if the bell is turned so that a long side faces him. A severely handicapped child may play his bell repeatedly, being unable to moderate his activity to take direction from you. It may help to hold his bell out of his reach until it is time for him to play, then present it to him and remove it after he has played. The musical experience that he can receive through this indirect control of his activity, as his bell sounds appropriately in the arrangement, may begin a more meaningful participation for him.

Your conducting will have to be decisive and detailed when introducing or teaching a new arrangement; it should become less directive and more supportive as the children become familiar with their parts. Adapt your leading to the response and abilities of each child with two main goals shaping your approach: to involve him in the way that will lead him best into experiencing the musical meaning of his activity, and to foster his responsive initiative.

Many of the methods of conducting instrumental group activities, described in the following chapter, apply to conducting resonator bell work.

76

Chapter Three

Instrumental Activities

Considerations of
the Therapeutic Effectiveness
of Live and Recorded Music

Through the use of instruments in group musical activities we work not only to activate handicapped children, but to deepen the mutuality of their participation in musically constructive activity. It follows, therefore, that live music, which can be flexibly adapted to suit the working situation, has a greater therapeutic potential than recorded music. The more severe the pathologies of the children the truer this is. Recordings can provide a range and variety of musical experience in the classroom, but for the purpose of supporting the active instrumental participation of handicapped children, they have severe limitations.

Every mechanical reproduction of music maintains its own tempo, regardless of the children's musical-rhythmic capabilities. In most circumstances, this makes recordings impracticable, particularly most commercially prepared recordings. For example, if a child can only play in one tempo or is unable to keep up with the music, or even time his playing of a single tone or beat so that it relates meaningfully to the music, his experience of both the music and his playing will be muddled. The experiential possibilities of the activity will not have been realized if what he hears and understands is confusing or unsatisfying. At best, no significant impression has been made upon him, and at worst, he is left with disappointment and frustration.

Even with children who may be able to work to recordings, there are still basic disadvantages. Each time a recording is used every musical element it contains is identically reproduced and reaches the children's minds as an exact duplication of previous experience. The result is that the children's responses to a recording tend to become habitual, and their playing or beating to it automatic; the functional relationship they form to the music is limited because it becomes fundamentally mechanical. Recorded music is not addressed, cannot be addressed, directly and at the moment to the children in musical activity. They cannot form a *living, working* relationship to it. It lacks the enlivening immediacy of human contact that you, as leader or musician, can provide.[1]

When *you* make the music, a working relationship can be created with the children that links you closely with their development. Your efforts, your perceptiveness, your care become united with their efforts, their experiences, and their achievements. The more you put your living self, with its warm feelings and good direction, into the work, the richer and more stimulating the children's experiences will be. In this closeness of participation music therapy takes on needed interpersonal dynamics and values.

The piano can give the greatest versatility in creating the musical support, continuity, and structure necessary for these kinds of instrumental activities. But the work need not be confined to piano—organ, accordian, and guitar (acoustic or electric) are rich in musical possibilities. For the therapist or teacher who plays none of these instruments, the Autoharp or Chromaharp is a relatively easy-to-play resource, capable of providing many attractive experiences. The full contribution of this instrument to music therapy and music in special education has yet to be realized.

The twenty-one chord model is recommended. Although it is easy to play with simple strokes, the Autoharp can also be played in a variety of colorful and interesting ways. Numerous rhythmic strum patterns can be used, strokes of different

[1]There will be situations in which the use of recordings is advantageous or necessary. In such circumstances the most successful solution is often to make your own recordings, or have them made by a colleague, specifically to suit the group you are working with, and the needs of your goal and style of presentation. For practical recommendations, see: Making Recordings, Appendix I, *Music for the Hearing Impaired—and Other Special Groups*, pages 404–409.

lengths played in rhythmic patterns, and the registers of the instrument used imaginatively—without overplaying the accompaniments. As with every instrument, the more proficient and resourceful the musician, the more she can bring and add to the children's instrumental work. The twenty-one standard chords provide a useful range of harmony, but for the harmonically adventurous, these possibilities can be widened. Should the therapist wish to have more harmonies available in the key in which she is working, the strings "accidental" to that key can be re-tuned to create secondary seventh chords—for example, in C Major, flatting all C#s, F#s, and G#s, and sharpening all D#s, changes the dominant sevenths on the 2nd, 3rd, 4th, and 6th degrees to secondary sevenths (the D7 becoming D minor 7 etc.). The Autoharp is greatly enhanced by amplification, particularly for use with larger groups or ensembles. For details on instruments and literature, see *Appendix 5*.

Although both the guitar and the Autoharp can be played melodically, they are most frequently used for harmonic and rhythmic accompaniment. For this reason, it is important that the voice, the most natural compliment to either instrument, provide the melodic element. Your voice may be used not only for songs, but for singing melodic lines nonverbally in instrumental music. In general, the use of the voice is to be encouraged in developing instrumental activities. The freedom and flexibility with which the work may be animated through your singing can be very effective.

Instrumental Activity Experiences

The Rhythm Band

Often, in the name of the "rhythm band," handicapped children are given an assortment of percussive instruments and encouraged to beat freely to music. This use of the instruments is frequently indiscriminate or haphazard and can give little in the way of musical or developmental experience.

The benefit of the rhythm band results from the organization of its activity. The class should be divided so that different types of instruments are grouped together, thus bringing about a contrast of several sections—one of drums, one of tambourines, one of triangles, etc. Each section plays to specific parts of the music, and perhaps all the instruments play together to give the composition a rousing conclusion. A piece of music or a song for this activity should be divided among the instruments in the most musical way possible: certain instruments can beat the basic beat; others, the melodic rhythm or accompaniment patterns; still others, accented beats or musical highlights. A suitable choice of music arranged with some inventiveness and led with verve can provide a variety of attractive musical activities that will challenge the children's attentiveness and give them pleasure and some basic musical-rhythmic experiences.

In the rhythm band the children beat time to music or outline its structure with percussion. This gives an experience of *following* or *accompanying* music. Almost always the music is complete in itself—it does not require the children's participation. Its rhythmic pulse leads, and its structure defines their beating, but essentially the children are *external to the music.* Their activity rarely has any part in creating the musical-tonal stimuli to which they are exposed. Hence their involvement is limited, and they cannot attain higher levels of active musical experience and the resulting satisfaction these can bring.

Another musically limiting aspect of rhythm-band work is that the children experience their own beating activity as much as they do the music. Repetitive beating is a strongly physical experience in which handicapped children often lose themselves, thereby losing the music, too, or feeling it merely as a stimulating accompaniment to their physical activity. The child who beats with enthusiasm and pleasure while totally unaware that he is not beating in time to the music is a familiar example of this. The same type of response can be observed in children beating, obsessively, basic beats or repetitive rhythmic patterns in the tempo of the music. An unremitting flow of patterned physiorhythmic activity obscures the sensitivities children have to the expressive qualities of melody and harmony, and to the communicative content and structure of music.

Deepening the Significance of Instrumental Work

The effectiveness of instrumental activity as music therapy can be increased by finding ways to open up the experiences of music to handicapped children, and to bring them into activity *within* music through the instruments they play. As very few of these children can use a conventional instrument with anything approaching normal skill, music instrument suppliers should be thoroughly explored for simple instruments that have effective musical possibilities for them. The children's playing of the instruments we choose or adapt to suit their abilities will naturally be limited, but it can be given genuine musical significance through the way in which it is set into an appropriate musical context. This will entail selecting, arranging, or composing music with the children's limitations in mind—using music exploratively to reinforce, yet heighten the meaning of, what they can play.

The part each instrument plays should be set in a composition so as to become *musically essential to it,* thus drawing the child who plays it into a specialized, but nonetheless real, making of music. Compositions can be arranged for a number of such simple instrumental parts so that they become components of a music unity. Each child's part, with its own musical meaning, will then become integrated into a total experience that will contain, and require, the work of all the children participating. An arrangement that carefully and inventively makes use of the various instruments' sounds can also serve to set off each part distinctly. This will make each child's efforts clear and his "music-making" will stand out in the combined work of the group.

Instrumental musical activities of this kind can create special situations in which we can intensify handicapped children's commitment and give them opportunities to develop perceptiveness, concentration, and initiative. Through consistently directed work they can experience purposefulness, perseverance, responsibility, and self-confidence—central and essential qualities for the growth of an integrated personality.

Instrumental arrangements of music will be discussed and illustrated following a consideration of the musical possibilities of those instruments that can be used effectively with handicapped children.

Musical Instruments

Each instrument possesses a character, a musical personality of its own that is created by its sound, its physical construction, and the way it is played. This individual quality gives each instrument its special musical value. Children quickly feel and respond to the character of an instrument we set before them. Through playing it and experiencing its sound, they can form a relationship to it that has musical purpose. Instruments should always be used so that (1) their individual characteristics stand out clearly in the music and (2) their different sounds complement or contrast each other. Each child who plays an instrument will then experience its musical character clearly, and through it become more conscious of the part he plays, and feel its meaning and importance in the total composition.

The better your equipment, the more confidently you can set up a music therapy program; the more assorted your equipment, the richer the variety of activities and experiences in which you can involve the children. Therefore, try to collect a wide assortment of instruments which produce good musical sounds, are sturdily built, and are attractive to look at.

Whenever possible, choose your instruments personally. Selections made solely through a catalog can be disappointing and waste funds. Take advantage of any opportunity—conference exhibit, showcase, workshop, any music store you can visit—to try out and gain first-hand experience of what is on the market. Only if you handle and play an instrument yourself and compare it with competing products can you be sure that you have made the best possible choice.

Drums and Tambourines

Although drums are mainly used in group musical activities for beating time and are therefore considered as rhythmic instruments, it should be remembered that every drum has its own timbre and produces a particular tone. Never think of drumbeating as a form of noise. Listen to the tones of your drums, become familiar with them, compare them, contrast them. Some drums have a solemn tone; others are mysterious; some are stern or ominous; others reverberate with warmth and energy. Listen, too, for the different qualities of sound that can be made by beating with strength or delicacy. Do not shrink from using powerful drums. There are often times in group musical activities when a real drum fortissimo is required, and when the music calls for it, the children should be encouraged to use strength freely. In contrast, it is a wonderful experience for a child to produce the beautiful sounds a powerful drum makes when beaten softly.

The choice of drums for musical activities should be determined by their differences in tone and sound quality and how

82

these vary with loud or soft beating. This will make the children's experience of the drum work you do with them more meaningful and dramatic.

The quality of a drum's sound depends upon the type of beater that is used. For this reason an assortment of beaters is desirable. Large drums usually require soft beaters, although a big drum with a heavy skin can take the harder and heavier mallet. Smaller drums need firm, lightweight beaters, or sticks. Wire brushes can be used to make thin, dry, or more delicate sounds. Different qualities of sound can be obtained from the same drum by the use of different beaters. Experiment to find the right combination of beater and drum for any piece of music. Very often a child's physical or emotional condition will also have to be considered in selecting the beater with which he will be able to do his best work.

If you have a snare drum, it is recommended that, for most purposes, the snare be removed. In vibrating against the lower head, the snare emphasizes the percussive impact of the beat. This can make the instrument too prominent and difficult to combine in a balanced ensemble unless played skillfully. Just slackening the snare away from the lower head often results in unwanted, distracting rattles. An alternative solution is to insert a strip of felt (or several folded paper towels) between the snare and the head and to tighten the snare. The resulting damping of the drum should be acceptable, and the snare retained for use when its characteristic dry, staccato sound is desired.

The timpani available for use in the Orff Instrumentarium have been designed for the purpose of playing bass notes in pitched percussion ensembles and are easily tuned to play clear, definite tones. They are invaluable when drum beats with strong tonal qualities are required for particular musical reasons. But for most percussive purposes they should be tuned out of the key or used selectively to avoid any domination of the music by an overinsistent repetition of bass tones.

Drums should have good quality parchment or plastic heads (skins). The rubber-covered variety of tom-tom, although a stopgap for a teacher who lacks better equipment, is musically unresponsive; it has little tone and is limited in its effect. Parchment heads will tend to slacken in humid weather. Tighten them as much as necessary to restore resiliency and tone, and slacken them off after the drums have been used. If a drumhead is excessively slack on the type of drum that cannot be adjusted, dampen the head and insert a thin packing of wood, or tuck a length of electric cord between the head and the drum case to take up the slack. Try to keep your drums in a closet at room temperature, never in a very warm atmosphere. If the closet is cold, bring the drums into the warmer room an hour or so before use.

A variety of drums is marketed by the suppliers listed at the back of this book. Other sources of drums that have both musical and visual color are the gift shops that import ethnic drums from various parts of the world. It is a great help to children if larger or odd-shaped drums are supported on stands so that the drumhead is about 20 inches above the floor.

Many of the remarks made about drums also apply to tambourines. You will find them very useful and colorful. Try to have two or more sizes on hand for different musical effects.

Tambourines are extremely useful and colorful in arrangements. They should be light enough to handle easily, with a firm percussive sound and a lively shake. Have two or more sizes available for different effects.

Cymbals and Gongs
Much fine therapeutic work can be done with a large orchestral cymbal—14 or 16 inches in diameter—mounted on a stand. Choose a cymbal with not too deep a tone which produces its high overtones clearly. It should make a stimulating "crash" that does not leave a persistent gonglike ring. The cymbal stand should be sturdy and bushed at the top with rubber or plastic tubing to prevent the cymbal from chattering against the metal stand; there should be sufficient felt pads above and below the cymbal to cushion it. Do not overtighten the wingnut—the cymbal should move freely on the stand.

A smaller, thinner cymbal about 10 inches in diameter is also useful and musically effective. This, too, should produce a brilliant "crash" and be free from any bell-like ring.

A pair of hand cymbals with a crisp brilliant timbre—not merely a dull clang—can be releasing and energizing. In joyous or triumphant music they help vivify the mood both in tone and action. They should be twelve inches or larger in diameter. As many children will have difficulty in controlling the cymbals with the loop handles usually supplied, it is recommended that these be replaced by wooden handles available from some percussion stores (the plastic loops supplied with them are unnecessary for classroom work and should be discarded).

A moderately sized gong can be especially attractive and

will impart drama and a sonorous quality to an arrangement. Avoid any gong that has too definite a tone as this may conflict with the tonality of particular pieces. In this regard, a light-weight gong will often be more versatile as its tone will not persist so strongly. A fourteen-inch gong on a simple metal stand will be a valuable addition.

Rattles, Shakers, Maracas

These should be chosen to combine a substantial sound, distinctive timbre, and lightness of weight. When used as rhythmic sound effects, they may be shaken freely and vigorously (as in "Bill's Train," page 33). Such unrestricted movements can be physically and emotionally satisfying for the motorically hand-icapped. But when used intentionally in scored arrangements, they gain in effectiveness, for example, when parts written for them begin and end on definite, preferably stressed, beats. Rattles and shakers that make an approximate musical tone can be used for delicate effects in songs and stories.

Blowing Instruments

Bird-calls that produce clear distinctive sounds are enormously attractive to children and are most effective in songs about birds, forests, parks, etc., or as sound effects in plays or stories.

Reed horns are vivid tonal instruments. They are simple to play and have proven to be a uniquely useful resource for instrumental activities with special needs people. In the sets that are commercially available, each horn's tone is produced by the reed in a pitch-pipe sounding a preselected tone. The horn's metal construction and the shape of the bell amplify the tone to give a full sound. A special pitch-pipe holder within the mouth-piece facilitates the changing of tones. A set of four horns plus sixteen interchangeable pitch-pipes can be arranged to sound any intervals or combinations of tones from the E above middle C to the G above the staff. They are lightweight, yet robust.

Children find the sound of the reed horns stimulating and satisfying. The directness with which the clear tone results from their blowing helps them learn to place their tones with con-scious intention. The controlling of breath necessary to play the horns loudly or softly, and to sustain tones, challenges the players' abilities and produces immediate musical results. They can be used very simply, for example, by replacing the resonator bells in "Swing Low," page 60, or in complex arrangements with other instruments as in "Oriental Night," pages 138–9. (See also *Appendix* 3, Reed Horns, Their Use and Maintenance.)

Simple flutelike instruments and whistles add a brightness of tonal color to musical arrangements. As the fingering of these instruments is almost always beyond the capabilities of severely handicapped children, adapt them so that each instrument plays a single tone. Having decided on the tone you will use, find which holes of the instrument need to be covered by the fingers in order to produce it. Cover these holes with tape so that the desired tone can be played without fingering. Two, three, or more flutes arranged to sound different single tones with musical clarity in a composition lead the children in a pleasing, successful way into simple tonal experience. Soprano and alto recorders may be used in this way. To obtain true tones, avoid overblowing.

The Melodica range of instruments requires more technical skill to play with musical discrimination but offers interesting possibilities for specialized musical activities with more capable or experienced children. If you wish to color-code or otherwise indicate specific tones, do not mark the keys directly—the markings may be impossible to remove. Make any marks on pieces of masking tape affixed to the keys.

It is important to keep blowing instruments in a hygenic condition, when used by many children. The most acceptable disinfectant seems to be Zephiran Chloride in a dilution of 1:750. Drug stores supply it either in this dilution or in a concentrate. It is odorless and tasteless. Simply moisten a cloth and wipe off the mouthpiece.

Stringed Instruments
Instruments to be bowed:
The use of bowed instruments—such as violins of various sizes and the cello—with moderately to profoundly mentally handicapped children or adolescents may seem somewhat demanding and out of place. But in music therapy, instruments have to be considered as means for providing musical experiences through which the children will benefit in specific ways. The warm, full tones of the cello and violins—tones that the player experiences as he performs the careful act of bowing—are unique. They bring a stirring quality of tonal experience into the scope of special musical activities.

To make it possible for handicapped children to use the violin and cello successfully, the instruments may be played with one string only, in the open position. This can be any one of the four strings tuned to suit the music, the other strings being removed. Older or more capable children, or those who have progressed from simpler musical activities, may be able to play on two open strings, or play other notes on a single string by fingering positions marked with tape on the finger board.

Violin strings may also be retuned to play a selected chord in the open position, for a child or adult to bow as a rolled chord in appropriate music. With this kind of tuning, the violin may become a "fiddle", being bowed rhythmically and freely, the strings played singly or in combination to produce a "hoedown" effect.

These instruments can bring a special mood of warmth and care into instrumental work. Many children will be fascinated by the sight of them and by the way they feel when held. Teach the players how to hold the instrument and to use the bow as correctly as they can. Although they will try hard to do this, many will be unable to do more than approximate it. Perfection here is secondary to the experiences they can gain from playing and hearing the sounds they make.

The violin and cello can also be played pizzicato (plucked). If used selectively in a musical arrangement, plucked strings will give the children a captivating experience.

The bowed psaltery is a further possibility. Soprano, alto,

and tenor models are available. This instrument is designed to play nineteen or more preset tones without the need for stopping strings. It is more complex to handle, requiring careful control, good eye-hand coordination, and a light bowing technique. Color-coding works well in designating specific tones. More capable children could use it to produce a variety of effects.

Instruments to be stroked, strummed or plucked:
The zither, the toy harp, and the lyre provide delicacy of tonal experience. They can be used harmonically by being tuned to suit harmonies in a composition and played in controlled glissandi. The breadth of lyric tone that results encourages the children to play them with attentive care. They can also be used melodically; using the fingers or a plectrum (pick), single tones, phrases, and simple melodies can be plucked. When they are combined with resonator bells, triangles, and other delicate instruments, charming and engaging music can result. Obtaining quality instruments of this kind is problematic—but not impossible, see *Appendix* 4.

The choice of plectrum affects both the timbre and the volume of strummed instruments. For most purposes, a soft flexible plectrum will produce full rounded tones—yet this should be firm enough to enable the child to apply sufficient pressure to produce a good volume. Often, a plastic plectrum with a layer of felt glued to each side, will best answer these needs. Should a brighter or stronger tone be required, use a plastic or metal pick.

The chordal dulcimer, developed in Great Britain for kindergarten and primary music education, is a simple harmonic instrument with a deep tone. Stretched over its sound box are twelve strings grouped in four sets of three, each set sounding one chord. It is normally tuned to play the tonic, supertonic, subdominant, and dominant triads in D Major, in the bass clef, but may be retuned to other chords. It is played by a beater that strikes three strings simultaneously, by a plectrum, or by the thumb or fingers. Single tones may be played if desired. (See photo, page 145.)

An Autoharp or Chromaharp is a very effective harmonic instrument.[1] Autoharps are widely available in many models

[1] The American-made Autoharp is preferable to the similar instrument exported from East Germany.

and sizes, from five to twenty-seven chords. These extremes of size are not recommended, a five-chord model gives only limited possibilities, and the twenty-seven chord model is overelaborate for most handicapped children and often insufficiently positive in operation. Fifteen or twenty-one chord models are the most practical and offer a good working choice of harmonies.

Autoharps are more technically challenging than the simpler instruments discussed above. They call for an extent of awareness and coordination that will be beyond the abilities of many children at first. Initially, some will only be able to stroke the strings while the therapist—or a classmate with the necessary strength and control—depresses the bar. But playing will bring its own motivation to master the technicalities; the instrument provides its own particular musical satisfactions. The sweep of the stroke provides a corresponding breadth of ringing harmonic tones—and the child who comes to feel the relationship of his tones to those of the piano and other instruments can derive a sense of security in his playing and be drawn deeply into the ensemble. The experience, too, of changing harmonies so decisively—of creating harmonic contrast and movement—and of supporting those playing other instruments, will give a player a real sense of musical capability.[1] The careful use of amplification will add to the instrument's presence.

Further harmonic possibilities lie in the guitar—and also in its relatives, the ukulele and the banjo. These are popular instruments and appeal especially to adolescents, though they hold many attractions for younger children who are capable of handling them. The technique in which a child strums a guitar while the therapist fingers chords and perhaps sings, is well suited to an individual setting, but is not so readily adaptable to the demands of group music-making. For this purpose the guitar is best retuned so that a child may play a chord successfully on open strings. The fullness of its tone can be very striking if the instrument is used selectively, for example, playing just in certain sections of an arrangement in distinct contrast to other instruments. The guitar lends itself well to special tunings, and, particularly with the use of the capo, offers a wide variety of harmonies from which to choose.

The baritone ukulele is more appropriately sized for young children, although its tone is not so full. It too can be retuned and used in the same way. On a ukulele tuned to a consonant

[1]See "Bolero" in *Music for the Hearing Impaired—and Other Special Groups*, pages 139–147.

89

chord, an able child can work for the satisfaction of changing harmonies by barring the chords—stopping all four strings together with one finger.

Bells

Bells that are struck:

Resonator bells contrast and/or blend well with most classroom instruments. Resonator bells with pitches both above and below the C′–G″ range of the standard sets marketed in the U.S.A., are available in the German equipment made for the Orff-Schulwerk instrumentarium. Chime bars (the British equivalent of resonator bells) have large tubular resonators and generally sustain their tones longer than most American or German bells: this is fine for slow music, but faster passages will require a damping technique.

Chord holders for resonator bells, such as those designed for the Tone Educator Bells, are a practical help in holding up to four bells securely with one hand. The holders are intended to hold bells arranged to play chords (and are supplied with special "fan" mallets), but are equally useful for holding bells playing simple melodic phrases. If only two or three bells are required, the holder can be filled out with other bells inverted, or with wood blocks cut to the same width.

A set of tubular bells is an imposing instrument that can take on special significance in the right musical context. Single tubular bells may be used with dramatic effect: the child who has the responsibility to play one tone, or several selected tones, at specific times in a composition, will be very conscious of the importance of his part.

Bells that are usually rung may be played by striking in some compositions or arrangements; a small hard mallet or a triangle striker is usually effective for this purpose.

Bells that are rung:

Handbells in two or more chromatic octave sets, offer an extensive freedom of choice for arrangements. A considerable outlay is involved in purchasing this equipment, but realistically, this is to be seen as an investment—an investment in the future development that is potential within those who will play them—in their latent musical intelligence, and in their capacities for personal and social growth. It is in fact an investment that will be repaid many times over by the lifetime service of the handbells, by the countless experiences

90

you will be able to create, and by the effort and commitment the players will invest in their music-making with them. Handbells are dignifying instruments to handle—for children and adults: the decisive action with which they are rung, and their clarity of tone, impart a special style to challenging, productive group work. Playing handbells also promotes a direct awareness in the players of how interdependent they are in music. Although they are usually played in ensembles needing no accompaniment, handbells may be used on a simpler level, with piano support, as resonator bells are. They can, for example, replace the resonator bells in most of the examples in *Chapter Two*. Handbells also combine effectively with other instruments in large and small ensembles.[1]

Attractive small bells can be obtained from gift shops or bazaars that import cast brass bells from India and the Orient. These come in different shapes and sizes with a variety of chimelike tones and are enjoyable for children to look at, hold and ring. Choose a number of bells with different pitches so that you have a selection for matching the keys of songs or compositions you are going to use.

Bells can be rung to sound with tones of the melody or harmony. They can be used to play complete simple melodies (one or two bells to a child), but are often more effective when used sparingly to play short phrases or single tones that (1) create a mood, (2) imitate, or make a contrast with, selected musical passages, (3) highlight important musical-dramatic moments. Examples of music using these principles are on pages 114 and 177–179. (This music was originally composed for a number of "gift shop" bells imported from India. Photo pages 180–181.)

Cow or mule bells, heavy brass bells from Greece, and sleigh bells can also be given places in appropriate musical arrangements.

"Melody bells," consisting of plastic bell-shaped resonators with small pressed metal bells mounted inside, have inadequate tone and timbre. Consequently, they do not offer much to this work.

---

[1]For an example of the use of handbells with other instruments and piano see "Oriental Night" by Herbert Levin, pages 138–9 and the score in *Music for the Hearing Impaired—and Other Special Groups*, pages 148–152.

Triangles

The therapeutic effectiveness of the triangle is greatly increased when it is suspended from a stand. A child can then apply himself to it with more control and precision, both in timing and dynamics. The triangle should not be used haphazardly but should make its clear musical statement to accent or enhance carefully determined moments of the musical experience, be they words, tones, or chords.

Metallophones and Xylophones

The metallophones and xylophones made for use in the Orff-Schulwerk are all attractive resources. In priority of choice, the first could be the alto xylophone, followed by the alto-soprano metallophone, then the bass xylophone. Chromatic instruments are necessary for complete freedom in arranging and composing. As the quality of these instruments varies considerably from one manufacturer to another, it is essential to compare similar models before finalizing a choice. For example, examine how well the adjustable damper works on the metallophone. It must be efficient in varying the sustaining of tone if you are to have control of harmonic and melodic clarity. Instruments with "overtone tuning" are to be preferred, their tones are richer and more capable of being sustained.

These are handsome instruments. Their strong clear sounds—the mellow fullness of the metallophone, the bright colorful tone of the xylophone—plus their size and construction, make a deep impression on both children and adults and set an expectant mood for musical work.

They may be used in a variety of ways: playing a glissando on the xylophone requires care, a quick movement of the arm and a fair amount of strength. To make this exciting sound at a telling moment in the music can be a freeing experience for a child who is timid in using his body. For the simplest parts, all the bars except those required can be removed—or just those adjacent to those that play, to define the part. Tones to be played may be designated with colored labels. If a number of different melodic phrases are to be played, they can be color-coded, each phrase in a different color. Such markings not only ensure the child's performance, they give her confidence and enable her to achieve a sense of personal success. Playing these instruments requires a deliberate, firm movement—the beater must be lifted immediately after striking the bar. This can be a real challenge for some individuals. Attentiveness to the music, physical effort and accuracy—these call for a coordination of aural and visual perception and muscular control that can be therapeutic for many handicapped children and adults. These instruments are very versatile in enabling a teacher or therapist to suit the complexity of a part to the present or growing abilities of players. Parts can be extremely simple and still be effectively set; for more capable players, melodic lines or harmonic intervals can be transferred from the piano part itself.

Individual rosewood resonator bars ranging in pitch from contrabass to soprano—also manufactured for the Orff-Schulwerk—have many applications, and give much the same freedom of choice and spatial arrangement as resonator bells.

The glockenspiel, if well made, with a strong clear tone, may be a useful part of an ensemble or provide lovely special effects in an activity. Avoid inexpensive metal "xylophones", which are not always accurately tuned and of limited usefulness.

Miscellaneous Instruments

Claves, wood blocks, tone blocks, "talking" or log drums, and similar instruments produce interesting percussive sounds, and can be effective if used for definite musical purposes. Handle-castanets give stimulating rhythmic effects. The guiro can be used both rhythmically and for sound effects. Although finger cymbals can be difficult for many handicapped children to manage, their tone can add an important highlight—provided they are of professional quality. Sand blocks provide effects in songs about trains, and more delicately, in songs about the sea or the wind. Jingle clogs and rhythm sticks receive limited consideration as musical instruments. They have their place as a means of physical rhythmic activity, but they have no musical sound to contribute to ensemble work, and are of little value for sound effects.

Music for Instrumental Work — Instrumental Scoring

The use of an instrument takes its musical significance from the music in or with which it is played, and the relationship the part it plays has to the music. This relationship can be rhythmic, melodic or harmonic, or any combination of the three. The timbre of each instrument is important in itself, yet it gains greater experiential effect from how it relates to the character of the music and to other instruments played in the same piece. Therefore, two basic considerations are of importance:

1. *Suitable music.* The music will be more effective if it has a well-defined quality. This can arise from a number of factors: a melody that has identity, and which is attractive or makes an impression; a clear rhythmic structure and form; a definite mood; an enjoyable sound character; and, in the case of a song, an idea that is attractive and comprehensible (or which may become comprehensible in the course of the work). The music must be so structured that it can accommodate instrumental parts, or have a content that can carry them.

2. *The way the instruments are scored.* The arrangement will naturally be more successful if the instruments are used effectively. Their timbres and/or tones must be expressively appropriate to the music, they must be placed in the melodic and rhythmic structure to add to the effect of the music—or to complete its effect. When several instruments are used, they must combine or contrast musically.

Series books and other song books published for regular school music programs have innumerable suggestions for using instruments. Many can be used, or adapted for use, with the handicapped. There are also instrumental activities published especially for the handicapped. All should be considered as possible resource materials which can be freely changed, simplified or elaborated to suit the needs and abilities of particular groups. It is a fact however, that at present, there is only a limited repertoire of compositions and arrangements available that aim to realize to a fuller extent the special developmental possibilities inherent in group instrumental activities. For this reason, a teacher or therapist who wishes to involve her children in such experiences is encouraged to make her own arrangements. This will mean exploring the possibilities of instruments as her children are able to play them, and of discovering in practical, experimental work, what can be meaningful, engaging, focusing, purposeful, and rewarding for them. This can become a creative adventure in music therapy.

One simple approach to scoring is to take a song the children enjoy and use instruments for sound effects as suggested by the words. Such sound-effect arrangements, made to illustrate the contents of seasonal or humorous songs can be interesting and fun to play. Instruments may also portray characters in narrative and songs belonging to stories (see the references to *The Three Bears* in the following pages).

Generally, the therapeutic effects of instrumental activities are deepened when the parts go beyond sound effects to take on greater *musical integrity* in the context of the piece, when they have the quality of *belonging to and in the music*.

Many spirituals and folk songs are suitable for arranging; often their words will suggest the best instruments to use to express the dramatic meaning of the text, or to deepen the mood. For example, "Oh, What a Beautiful City!" arranged for reed horns and cymbals; "Go Down, Moses!" with softly played drums and a gong; "Camptown Races" for clappers, rattles and whistles, become enlivening, expressive experiences. Such arrangements stimulate and challenge the players, and arouse the others in the group, awaiting their turns, to sing with more enthusiasm.

Show tunes and popular songs—those with memorable melodies and suitable words—lend themselves well to arrangements for older players. Compositions taken from the classical repertoire can be successfully used as a basis for instrumental activities.

Music Composed for Handicapped Children

Music especially composed for this kind of instrumental work must make a strong musical impact. Effective therapeutic work that is going to search for, discover, and, hopefully, realize untapped potentials in handicapped children must reach beyond the superficial response. Music composed for this purpose must be truly musical, not necessarily in the sense of high aesthetic standards, but in that it possesses *musical vitality and clear, free, expressive character*. Within the general conditions of pathology in which it is used, it must be capable of arousing an emotionally significant response and of maintaining and increasing the intensity of this response despite the innumerable repetitions music therapy will require.

Handicapped individuals of different ages and conditions present different needs; the emotional content of the compositions will need to be suitable to each group; the range of abilities found in groups of both children and adults will call for gradations of complexity in instrumental parts. Whatever the quality of the music, or the character of the instrumental parts, they should always be an expressive, functional unity.

Examples of the Use of Instruments

Arrangements and compositions for young children should be simple yet colorful. Often the more sparingly the instruments are used, the better.

An arrangement of "Joshua Fought the Battle of Jericho" for five children playing three tuned horns, a cymbal, and a drum shows that striking musical effects can be obtained with an instrumental simplicity that lies within the abilities of younger handicapped children.

A quiet, solemn beginning sets the initial mood of the song, the middle section becomes dramatic, and the arrangement finishes with a stirring climax.

Jer - i - cho, _ *etc.* and the walls came tumb - ling down!

Up _ to the walls _ of *etc.* "Go blow those trum-pets, those trum-pets," those

The following five illustrations are from an instrumental adaptation of the story of "The Three Bears.*"The 18 instrumental parts in the composition were developed in experimental work with retarded children to be within their comprehension and to give their abilities scope for development. The work is suitable for a wide age range of children.

"The Owl's Song" uses three single-toned flutes and a tunable whistle selectively. The unity of music, instrumental parts, and story, illustrated here, makes each child who plays an essential participant in the music and story making, regardless of the simplicity of his part or the limitations of his abilities.

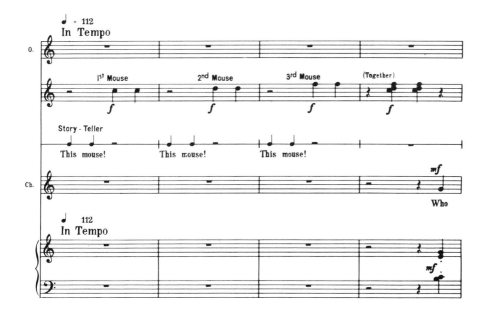

"The Birds' Song" uses three bird calls and a tunable whistle. The musical significance of these parts for the children results from the attractive, clearly differentiated sounds of the instruments and from their active roles as characters in the song and story.

Night - in - gale, The Pee - wit, the Cuck - oo, the Night - in - gale all

lived in the woods with the Owl. The Pee - wit, the Cuck - oo, the

101

"The Bears' Song" is written for cello, violin, and quarter-sized violin, each with one open string. The illustration shows how the instruments can be most simply used and yet be musically true and engaging in their effect. The tonal contrast of the instruments heightens the characterizations of the three bears they represent.

Look-ing out the win-dow was a Ba - by Bear, A lit - tle

bear. A naugh-ty bear. 2) Look-ing out the win-dow was a Ba - by

Bear, A lit - tle bear, A naugh-ty lit-tle bear. Look-ing, look-ing,

Baby Bear

Father Bear

look-ing at his fa - ther dig - ging!

A lyre, tuned pentatonically, is used to represent the character of Goldilocks; that she has a Shadow, represented by a toy harp, tuned diatonically, adds the interest of musical interplay to the song. The instrumental parts consist of ascending and descending glissandi. The harp imitates the lyre throughout, except once in each verse when it serves to prepare for the return of the main phrase of the song by reversing the direction of a glissando. This expressive change, in what would otherwise be a continuous imitation, becomes surprisingly important to the children. The tonal qualities of these instruments have a sweetness that the song enhances. This gives the children the chance to create a lyrical mood through their playing, an experience that is rare for them.

G.

Sh.

Ch.

Shad-ow.   When she hopped   her Shad-ow hopped!   When she skipped
Shad-ow.   When she jumped   her Shad-ow jumped!   When she danced

her Shad-ow skipped!   Gold - i-locks had   a   Shad - ow.
her Shad-ow danced!   Gold - i-locks had   a   Shad - ow.

105

Experimental work during the early development of "The Three Bears."
The little blond girl is too hyperactive to hold the Nightingale bird-call,
but she is excited by its warbling trill and wants to blow it. At the right
moments in the song the therapist presents it to her. Interest is shown by

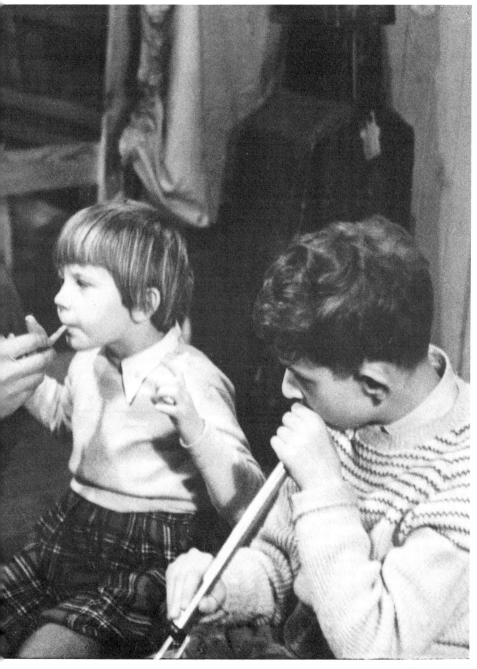

the Cuckoo and Owl players; the Owl's part comes next and he is ready to play. The girl, on the left, who plays the Pee-wit, is disinterested; she is one of the three children, out of approximately eight hundred, who showed no positive response to music.

Baby Bear is all enthusiasm for his part in the story. He is engrossed in
the action of bowing the instrument and the tone it creates. That his
tempo is his own and not the music's does not matter at this point, it is
achievement enough to have been able to include him in the general

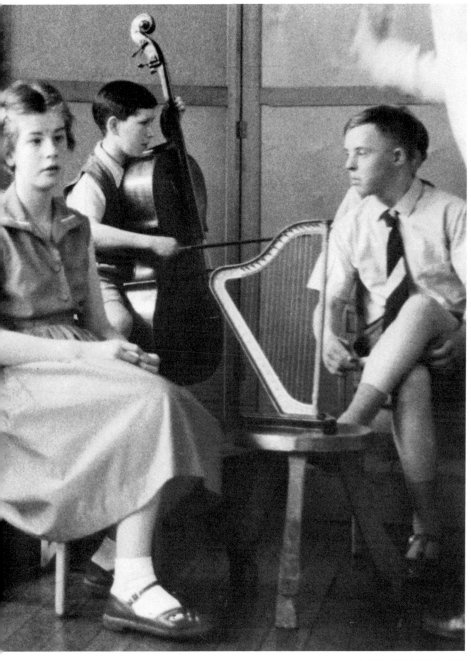

order and purpose of the composition. Mother Bear feels responsibility, she wants to play correctly and works with the conductor. Father Bear knows his part perfectly and needs no direction. Goldilocks' Shadow awaits her part in her song.

As Goldilocks' Shadow plays in "Goldilocks Had a Shadow" the Bears watch her. She was a sweet, compliant, but easily confused child. Belong-

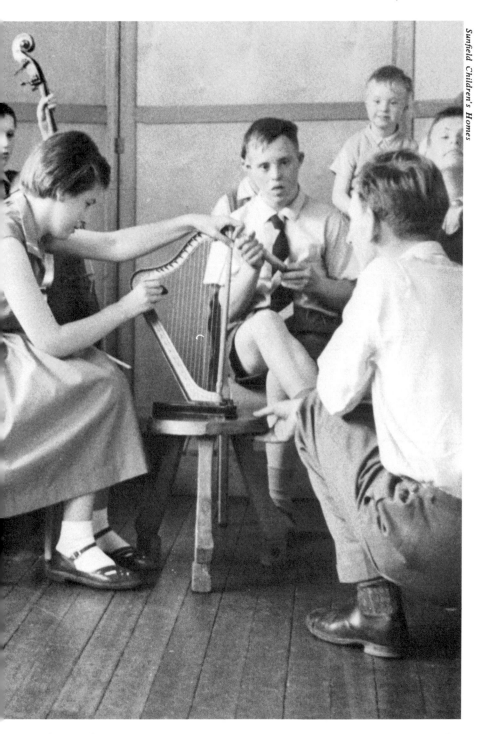

ing to the orchestra, the success of her playing, and the character of the musical experience gave her a center of quiet confidence.

111

The cymbal in this song represents the Sun. The careful, controlled crescendo, played by the child on this instrument—from *pppp* to *ffff*—creates a dramatic experience. The free, expressive setting of the words to alternate measures of 3/4 and 4/4 adds life to the song and keeps the cymbal player alert; he cannot beat semi-automatically at regular intervals but must listen to and be conscious of the irregular measure structure and adapt his cymbal beating to it as he makes the crescendo.

A demonstration performance of "The Three Bears." The standing boy sings as he carefully makes the long, gradual cymbal crescendo in "The Sun Is Rising." Most of the children are singing vigorously; the presence of an audience has not disturbed the working spirit.

"Mary and Joseph's Music" from "The Children's Christmas Play" illustrates how small handbells can be used to play phrases that extend and sustain a melodic structure. Their tonal qualities, in conjunction with the piano part, create an appropriate mood.

(During the music, Joseph leads the Donkey on which Mary is seated up the center aisle to a position immediately before the stage.)

See also the use of bells to delineate a melodic-harmonic line in the first section of the "Overture" to "The Children's Christmas Play" (page 177).

114

Lord, let me live as I will!
I need a little wild freedom,
A little giddiness of heart!
For whom else are your mountains?
Your snow wind? Your springs? . . .

From "The Prayer of the Mountain Goat."[1] The music is virile and rhythmic, the instrumental parts bold and often syncopated, and the words—the boys found them fun to sing—are full of imagery. The work was challenging for this educable class. The boys had little concept of structured, controlled playing at first. They could only find out what this could achieve by gradually accepting the discipline and order it required. The work was not easy, but the boys grew to be very fond of their music, and proud of their capabilities as a group. They gave several performances of this piece and of other settings from *Prayers From the Ark*. The boy in the center sang a special part, added to include his beautiful voice.

[1]*Prayers From The Ark*. Poems by Carmen Bernos de Gasztold. Translations by Rumer Godden, Music by Paul Nordoff. © Copyright 1983 by Theodore Presser Co.

A group of hearing impaired students concentrate intently in a music class. All are profoundly deaf, except the severely deaf boy beating the drum. All enjoy music and have done so consistently since the program began two years earlier. They are working on an instrumental arrangement of "Kum Ba Yah" *(Spirituals)*, following large charts showing their parts in colored picture notation. The basic structure of the work is simple, complexity builds up, step by step, through repetition and addition. The instruments' sounds contrast clearly. The students' hearing aids make a great deal of music accessible to them, and through their intent work they are activating their capacities for musical-auditory processing. A year later, members of this group were writing that music was "good hearing" and "beautiful sound."

(Because a student teacher is working with the class, the leader takes the opportunity to play one of the instrumental parts. This is instructive as it gives an "inside" experience of the arrangement as it sounds and is structured relative to that particular instrument. A therapist can gain insight into the experiential significance the part holds for a player.)

and the Versatility of Materials

" . . . oh Lord, kum ba yah." Men of Marbridge Ranch, Texas, are equally intent as they work on the identical arrangement. As not all can follow charts, their playing is being directed. The tambourine and Melodica orchestrate the first verse, resonator bells and a cymbal are added in the second, a reed horn and a triangle join in the third, and so forth. Each instrument has precise parts to play. Exactly the same characteristics that engaged the hearing impaired students appeal to these normally hearing, mentally handicapped men: an enjoyable warm song, clear structure, playing attractive instruments, producing a rich variety of sounds, active experiences of rhythm, musical contrast and organization, and belonging to a group with a special responsibility. Some weeks later, the men performed "Kum Ba Yah" as part of the musical offering at the ranch's Anniversary Program.

The rich cultural heritage of the Spirituals offers a unique source of experience and activity to music therapy and music in special education. There are many reasons why this should be so: The repetition in the lines and melodies of most Spirituals makes them relatively easy to assimilate, and provides security. The language is simple, yet direct and meaningful. Often, special needs people respond to the heartfelt honesty of a Spiritual and feel an affinity with its mood or content. Almost always there is a natural expressiveness in the combining of words and melody that makes them satisfying to sing. Spirituals have a special personal quality that brings them humanly close, their melodies have character and live in the memory. They appeal to a wide age-range; the same Spiritual may be simple enough for young children to enjoy, yet possess the maturity or dignity that adults will relate to. There is hardly another single body of song literature that offers so much.

Both young adults have been playing in the resonator bell parts of "All Night, All Day" *(Spirituals)*. As they watch the Autoharp player practicing, Bill sings along with the Spiritual. Lack of fine and gross muscular control has always prevented him from playing an instrument successfully, but the "piano-action beater" enabled him to be part of the ensemble. (See pages 242–243 for details of the piano-action beater.) In later sessions, using this same adaptive device, he was able to play the gong part in this arrangement—he was so effective with this that the piano hammer had to be fitted with a small mute of plastic foam.

"All Night, All Day" is scored for five resonator bells, reed horn, Autoharp (replacing the chordal dulcimer), triangle, and gong. After the opening with bells and horn alone, the gong plays on the first note of the melody. The Autoharp then plays a series of chords, one in each of the next four measures. It was particularly important for the cerebral palsied girl who played the Autoharp that her chords came after the melodic tones (on the offbeats). In this way she had the words and melody to guide her, yet her playing came through strongly and made an effective contribution to the music. This gave her both confidence and pleasure. She also had the possibility of feeling that she was "keeping the beat going" as she stressed the second beats. The buttons of the chords she used were color-coded and she was able to work from a simple color-coded pictorial chart, pointed out to her by an aide. She worked hard and was proud of her role in the piece.

All Night, All Day

Now I lay me down to sleep. Angels watching over me, my Lord.

411-41044

The more each instrumental part stands out as a colorful, essential part of the music, the more effectively it can be used to promote the development of handicapped children. In each instrumental part the teacher can focus the child's concentration upon his activity; as she supports his work her attentive encouragement becomes therapeutically effective. The musical meaningfulness of his part captures the interest of the other players and of the children who are watching and listening. They participate to an ever-growing extent in his efforts and achievements and are moved to work as intensively when their turn comes. A group dedication develops that progressively unites everyone in the spirit of the total activity.

Work in the classroom on "Three Hairy Furry Bears" (a march with repeated rhythmic motifs and horn parts). Individual concentration and mutual interest combine to make a lasting experience for everyone. The

Schima Kaufmann, Philadelphia

children seated know they will have their turns at playing; they learn as they listen and watch. The good working atmosphere unites us all.

123

Working with the Children

The therapeutic effectiveness of instrumental group activities depends not only on the music and instruments used but also on adequate preparation for the work. The pianist should be thoroughly familiar with the score; the leader must learn the music and every child's part. The instruments should be prepared for each session. At least one preparatory meeting should be arranged by the team members in order to go through the work they are going to use before presenting it to the children. Both should be in agreement on all details so that their working together will be as skillful and efficient as possible. This will give their teamwork the assurance necessary for imparting beneficial experiences to handicapped children.

Playing for Instrumental Activities

The pianist will not only be playing for the children but will be sharing with them the experience of making music. She should not think of herself as merely accompanying children's activities, but as creating the ordered world of music that makes their activities meaningful. Their learning how to listen to the music with which they play their instruments will depend largely on how she plays hers. All their experiences will be heightened when their music is played with directness and clarity.

Do not play with "personal" feeling; subjective feelings should never influence playing for this work. This does not mean that you should not enjoy the music. On the contrary, you will find a greater pleasure in it through the attitudes and intentions that can really "live in your fingers" as you play. The rise and fall of melodies, played with a feeling for the "space" between each tone, the awareness of each harmonic change, an interest in the relationship between the number of beats in each measure, and the rhythms of the melodic phrases that span several measures will all make the music more living for you. Your playing, then, will not be motivated by the way the music makes you feel; rather, your knowledge of all that is happening in it and your own pleasure in playing it will be directly communicated to the children. This will change your playing from a personal expression into making music for therapy. It will always be related to the children's abilities and needs when you are in close rapport with them and your attention is focused on

124

their activities. This is possible only when you know the music so well that you do not need to give the score more than cursory attention. A pianist who must keep her eyes on the page all the time will never really be sure of what the children are doing, and it will be difficult for her to maintain the close working relationship with the leader that is essential to therapy.

Adapt your playing perceptively to meet the constantly changing circumstances and situations of the work. You may often have to make a pause, for instance, to ensure a child's proper entry in the music. This will enable him to feel the music fitting around his activity and so to become increasingly sure of the musical sense of his part. If, from the beginning, the children feel that the music will "wait for them" and then support them, they will relate more deeply to it. Tempos should never be mechanical, yet they must be firm enough to keep the basic beat alive; a tempo can change to very slightly faster, or to very slightly slower—at musically appropriate times—without any loss of the beat. Tempos may have to be varied—slowed for a child who cannot, in the beginning, play with vitality, or speeded up to the quick tempo in which another child is only able to play. Make the ritard at the end of a piece when it is musically right to do so. The children will feel the rightness of this and enjoy making it with you.

One group of children may need an emphasizing of the underlying basic beat. When you provide this, be sure that you do not sacrifice clarity of melody or harmony. Another group may make important responses to the melody; in bringing out this element, do not lose the pulse of the basic beat.

Never play so loudly that you cannot hear the children playing, or so softly that they cannot hear you. Dynamics should always be musically appropriate even though you may have to ex- aggerate *fortes* and *pianos* from time to time in order to bring them to the children's attention.

Pedal each chord so that it is "clean," that is, free of any tones belonging to the preceding chord. Use the pedal sparingly in any case—more frequently for lyric music, and for soft, slow music, but hardly at all for rhythmic, jaunty, gay music. When music is blurred by overpedaling the various emotional and ex- periential effects that its melodies and harmonies can have upon the children will be marred. After an intensive period of work it is often wise to change the working mood and relax the children. You can do this by playing a rousing song every- one knows, or some piano solo, different in character from the

Sunfield Children's Homes

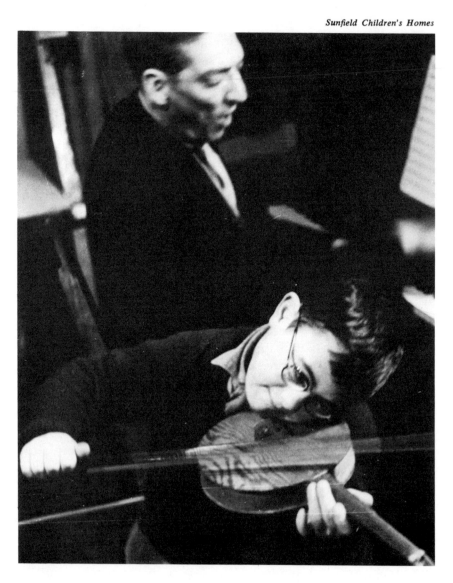

Responses to the Character of Instruments

Adults are equally responsive to the character of the instruments they are given to play. The same important considerations of quality, sound character, musical effectiveness, and variety apply. The effort and concentration of the player are directly enhanced by the effectiveness of the instrument's sound in its musical context. This also stimulates the attentiveness of the others in the group—see the photo—the triangle player appreciates her friend's success with the reed horn, the Melodica player joins in directing the part.

The musical instruments a therapist has to offer her clients, both children and adults, form an essential part of her professional equipment. They are

tools of the trade. Every professional and craftsman is dependent on the specific equipment of his trade to carry out his work, and cope with the variety of its situations consistently and competently. The music therapist who must make do with limited equipment is limited in the nature of the stimulation she can provide, the quality or intensity of the experiences she can generate, and scope of the activities she can lead. Conversely, the better, more varied, and complete her equipment, the more resourcefully can she work in a variety of settings, and the more effectively and creatively can she use her skills for the enrichment and benefit of her clients.

129

music you have been using. Everyone will enjoy this and be refreshed when work is resumed. It becomes possible to engage the children for 45 minutes to an hour or more, particularly as the work advances and the group becomes a unity, working in larger structured activities. Such a unity of handicapped children can function on a high and truly musical level of intelligence and achievement.

You will have to play the same music over and over again. This is another reason why the music should be fine in quality, for it must stand up to innumerable repetitions. Even so, no repetition is the same. The children keep the music alive as they respond progressively to it, experience it more fully, and master their instrumental parts. Your involvement in them and in the progress they make—not only in music but, through music, in personality development and behavior—keeps the music always fresh for you.

Leading Instrumental Activities

It is to the children's advantage that they get the most direct experiences possible of the music, of the instruments they use, of themselves in activity, and of their classmates working with them. For this to happen they need the functional security your leadership can give them when you have a good working knowledge of your material.

Do not be discouraged if you have had little or no musical training and are unable to learn the song or piece from the printed score; ask your teammate or a musical friend to play it for you. Copying the words of unfamiliar songs can impress them upon your memory. When memorizing the orchestral parts of a composition imagine the players in their places around you, sing the song or music to yourself, and practice the conducting of each child's part. You will find this of practical assistance.

While you are learning the music and the parts, try to imagine the new musical experiences you will be bringing to the children. For example, if you are working with "The Bears' Song" from "The Three Bears," know the song so well that you can sing it through to yourself and hear, in your imagination, the three instrumental parts. Feel what a musical pleasure it is when Father Bear, as the cello, makes his first entrance in the song. The deep note of the cello has a rich, warm, and robust sound. Imagine what fun this is for a child to play, what a bold thing it is for him to do. The small-sized violin, Baby Bear, plays immediately after Father Bear. The musical contrast is

130

captivating. The thin, high sound of a small violin has charm and musical humor. There is gaiety in the way it matches the words of the song. A little later, when Baby Bear and Father Bear play together, the musical interest of the song quickens. Then Mother Bear makes her entrance. This is a happy moment for the children because now all three instruments are in the music, all Three Bears in the song. Feel how the soft, gentle tone of the violin in the middle register contrasts with the other instruments, and how it suits Mother Bear's character. When they all play together, a few measures later, it is both a dramatic experience and a thrilling sound. The concluding phrases of the song, with the three instruments playing on every beat, are full of jubilation.

If you can feel in this way the musical life, the expressive content of the music you work with, you will be awake in your feeling to each musical, dramatic event at the moment it occurs. You will conduct the children and bring in their different instrumental parts with a lively awareness of all that is happening. This will communicate to the children. Your conducting, your whole manner with them, will be alive and musically creative.

Preparations for Work; Introducing the Instruments

Arrange the largest clear space possible in the room. The piano should be placed so that the pianist has an unimpeded view of this space. Chairs for the group should be set in a semicircle or a large horseshoe with one end near the piano. The instruments should be ready for use and at hand.

When the children are seated, sing greeting songs to enliven them and set a good working mood before introducing the work you are going to do. As this should be a special experience from the beginning, be inventive and arouse the warmth of the children's interest by your mode of presentation. When you bring out the instruments spend some time introducing each one to the class, so that the children experience its quality and hear its sound. If the instruments belong to a story, tell little anecdotes that create a picture around each one and the character it represents to deepen the children's involvement in the work and in the parts they are to play.

When beginning work on a new piece of music or a song it is usually better to choose the instrumentalists from the more capable children, for they will help you to get it into good shape more easily; the others will have the opportunity to become familiar with the composition as you repeat it and may begin to learn it as they watch and listen.

The instrumentalists should be placed within the horseshoe or semicircle where the pianist will be able to see the face of each child and also the way he plays his instrument. The rest of the class should have as good a view of the players as possible. Give out each instrument in turn and let the players try them. Work on the methods of playing the instruments and when the children have enough proficiency to carry them into the first attempt, introduce the music and guide their playing of the parts through your conducting. In this way the children experience the music and the musical meaning of their parts as a unity from the beginning. Their participation then has a deeper musical origin.

Conducting and Directing

The clarity and intensity of the children's experiences depend upon the skill of the conductor. When a work is new and the children need much guidance, or when a severely handicapped child tries to master a part that is a critical challenge to him, the conductor should use her skill to lead through and beyond the difficulties of pathology into successful achievement. The conducting of handicapped children in group instrumental activities comprises many special techniques. Almost every leader will develop her personal style of conducting, yet its effectiveness and impact will depend upon an ability to cope with the varied and often unique circumstances that belong to this work. Some of the basic techniques helpful for efficient conducting are discussed below.

Work at the children's eye level. As the children are often seated to play their instruments, it is awkward for them to play if they have to look up to follow the conductor's directing. Kneel before them to be at their eye level, nearer to them and to their instruments. Not only is this much more comfortable for them, but it brings you into a closer working connection and expresses your intentions. Children find this stimulating and encouraging; they take their musical work seriously and come into a good working relationship with you. The kneeling position also enables you to use your upper body freely as you conduct. If this position is uncomfortable, conduct from a low chair.

132

Do not let your own response to the music lead you into beating time with big movements of your hands. Limit your natural rhythmic response to small movements of your shoulders, hands, or head. Keep decisive movements for conducting the instruments. If you turn to lead the singing of the class while the instruments are not playing, you will need to use somewhat larger gestures. But here, too, do not indiscriminately beat time; use your movements to emphasize important notes in the melody, important words in the song, and the rhythmic settings of the words.

Use large, vital movements of your arms for leading the instrumentalists, especially when you are beginning work on a new piece. Be precise in these movements and adapt them to suit the instruments you are conducting. For example, use sideways movements of your arms and hands for the bowing of a violin or cello, and up-and-down movements for the beating of a suspended cymbal.

Use your hands independently and flexibly. When you are conducting two children playing instrumental parts that interweave or alternate, direct a child with each hand. If necessary you can use a gesture with one hand to "hold" one child from playing while you conduct the other with the other hand. The "holding" gesture is usually quickly understood when made with the palm of the hand. If you wish many players to play together, use both arms in wide, encompassing gestures. For loud playing conduct with assertive movements, perhaps even with a clenched fist. For softer playing gentle movements made with the open hand will convey the right feeling. When finger movements are used descriptively be sure they are precise. The movements of the wrist should always be rhythmically deliberate and telling.

Frequently a clear preparatory upbeat will be needed to bring in the children at the right time in the music. The upbeat takes the children into their preparatory movements before playing—drummers raise their sticks, horn players take a breath, and string players position their bows or plectrums on the strings. Movements for the upbeat will often have to be big. Raise one hand when conducting one child, both hands when conducting several children, and at the same time lift the upper body from the knees if you are kneeling, or from the waist if you are seated. Make these commanding movements clearly for they must arouse and poise the children for playing. The upbeat is particularly important in conducting a strongly rhythmic

Working on "What Is Music Made Of" by Herbert Levin
Working on the harmony section using different combinations of vari-

ously toned bells. The players follow direction closely and experience the succession of harmonies their bells create with the piano's support.

work, as it prepares and helps the children to play with rhythmic accuracy.

Children who have little rhythmic perception or rhythmic confidence, or those whose rhythmic sense is obscured by the uneasiness they feel when challenged by instrumental activity, require particular guidance. Some have a marked time lag and will always play late, others are so tense they "jump the gun" and play too soon. Adapt your upbeat to the difficulties and needs of each child. Try to judge how much time a "late player" needs to follow your direction. Signal him just this much in advance of when he is to play so that his instrumental entrance will occur at the right time in the music. Give the child who "can't wait" a very short cue or combine your upbeat with a holding gesture, releasing him at the exact moment he is to play. Such techniques can enable arhythmic children to hear and feel the rhythmic relationship between the parts they play and the music. They can begin to experience the musical meaning of their parts, find security in playing them, and the time can come when they will no longer need special direction.

When working on rhythmic patterns with a child who is rhythmically uncertain, conduct each beat with emphasis. If a child tends to continue beating after the pattern, make the last conducting movement of the pattern emphatic, and when your arms have reached the downward position freeze to complete stillness. Do not move until you raise your arms for the upbeat that precedes the next repetition of the pattern. Exaggerate your movements and make them angular if necessary. Once the child is beginning to beat the pattern return to more normal conducting.

If the child is beating a drum and is so handicapped that he is unable to follow direction and cannot check his beating to form a rhythmic pattern, reach out and "catch" the unwanted beats in the palm of your hand. Then he will be hearing, at some level of consciousness, the correct pattern in its relationship to the music and he may begin to form an idea of the rhythmic structure. Speaking the rhythmic pattern may help a child to grasp it. Use the rhythm of his name if it fits the pattern or any everyday speech phrase that is rhythmically correct: "How are *you*?," "Hello," "Good *Morning*," etc. Some chilren can pick up a pattern through a physical experience of it. This can be given by tapping the rhythm on knee, shoulder, or palm of the hand with a drumstick.

136

The mobility of your face enlivens your conducting. When in the working moment, you are living in a child's playing of his part, your face will express your perception of his efforts and your quick understanding of *his* understanding of what is happening. Music flows by in time and the children's activities and experiences follow quickly one upon another. Your facial expressions become spontaneous communications to them about each event as it passes; they express your purposeful attitude and keep the working relationship alive. Children can find assurance, encouragement, humor, and unspoken congratulations in the natural expressiveness of your face.

You will often find it necessary to use your eyes indicatively when conducting. If both arms are occupied in conducting two children's work, a directed look toward the child who is next to play, or a telling exchange of glance, will enable him to prepare for his part. At other times you may have to hold children in readiness with your eyes while your hands are busy and then use a movement of your head to bring them in. Eyes can often speak more explicitly than the voice during musical activities; the character of your glance can serve to stimulate or steady a child when the concentration of the working moment leaves no time for speech.

Adapt your conducting to the children's progress. As you repeat and build up the various instrumental activities, and as the children get to know them, the character of your conducting should change. When a child begins to master his part, to make his musical entrances with consciousness and courage at the right moments, support rather than lead him. Allow *his* initiative and perceptiveness, *his* memories and understanding to come to expression. But never withdraw your attentiveness; children must always feel you are there, poised to give assurance, affirmation, or guidance whenever necessary.

When a story is used as the basis for instrumental activities, it is often necessary for the leader to be the story-teller as well as the conductor. Stories should be told with vitality, imagination, and a broad range of vocal inflection. When the story-teller narrates to instrumental accompaniment, the volume and quality of her voice should be well adjusted to the character of the sound made by the instruments. If rhythmic speech is used by the narrator, it should be precise in accent and tempo. The story-teller's voice will be more effective, dramatically and musically, when it is freed from the casual inflections of everyday speech and used deliberately as a "narrative instrument."

Part of the School District of Philadelphia's All-City Orchestra of Trainable Children rehearsing for a demonstration concert under the direction of Herbert and Gail Levin.

The orchestra has been created for the most musically advanced trainable children in the school system. From ten schools they are bussed once weekly to a central location to work together on compositions written especially for them by Dr. Levin.

The instrumental arrangement of each piece of music is made to suit its expressive character; the instruments are chosen carefully, their tonal qualities explored, and parts written for them that combine or contrast their sounds in musical unity. The children's concentrated work realizes colorful orchestral experiences while giving them a strong sense of ensemble. In the photograph the children are shown working on a composition in an Oriental idiom; those on the front row have played the

School District of Philadelphia

theme of the A section on handbells in an Oriental scale. In the B section, struck handbells, triangle and gong accompanied a pentatonic melody on the piano—the xylophone played a counter melody to a repetition. Now, in the C section, horn players sound a rhythmic succession of fifths, punctuated by the cymbal. A return to the A section will conclude the performance.

The quality of fulfillment the children experience stems from the purposefulness of their work together. This purposefulness results from, and is sustained by, the fine quality of the instruments they play and the genuine musicality of their work. Social maturity has also resulted from the project, manifesting in confidence, enhanced self-evaluation, cooperativeness, and more consciousness of the importance of such things as personal grooming and deportment. Audiences have been consistently impressed by the high standard of the children's performance, and by their concentration and pleasure.

139

"Fun for Four Drums" with Finnish Children

The children are playing a single beat each, in succession, to the refrain:

Rummutetaan! Rummutetaan!   (Let's beat the drum!

Yks ja, yks ja, yks ja, yks!   One by one by one by one).

Example:

Martikainen, Majalampi Suomi-Finland

The whole group of 16 adolescents was totally unaccustomed to using *musical purpose*. As they took turns in *Fun for Four Drums* they had to learn to watch the leader and to take direction, they had to develop a concept of structured, rhythmic instrumental activity on this simple level. Now, after seven sessions, the activity form is established, and they are becoming interested in each other's parts.

Up to this point, the work has been taught in its simplest form: each drum part as a separate entity, divided from the others by repetitions of the refrain. The therapists are beginning to take the work a stage further by teaching the planned interplay of parts, whereby one person's pattern and music alternates with the patterns and music of the others. This creates musical-rhythmic contrast and interest, which stimulates and demands increasingly conscious participation.

141

In the course of the work, each child beats a simple rhythmic pattern, a musical rhythmic *idea* that he must try to remember, to a section of music.

Drum 1, nearest the camera, played by a retarded, emotionally disturbed girl, plays on the fourth beat in every measure of her music.

Example:

The spastic boy on Drum 2 must make a considerable effort to beat the two answering beats his music calls for.

Example:

The music for Drum 3 requires three beats. Olavi has to concentrate not to beat four or five.

Example:

Helena has the large Drum 4. She needed three sessions, once weekly, to master the rhythmic idea of this part.

Example:

The refrain which began the composition is repeated between each child's drum solo and at the end, unifying and structuring the experience.

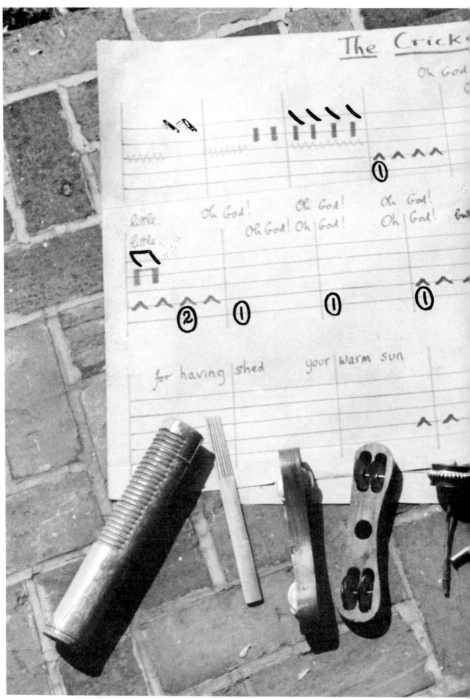

A setting of "The Prayer of the Cricket," from *Prayers from The Ark,* by Carmen Bernos de Gasztold, translated by Rumer Godden. Reproduced by permission of Macmillan and Co., Ltd., The Macmillan Company of Canada, Ltd., and the Viking Press, Inc. Copyright 1962, by Rumer Godden.

Oh God!
Oh God! I am very little
little little
little
you have set
thank you thank you
Thank you
Then take, then
Thentake, then

The instruments of "The Prayer of the Cricket," and the instrumental score prepared for a group of educable girls.

The instruments each have their own line in the system; in their order from left to right they are notated on the score from top to bottom. The notational symbol for each was derived, as far as was possible, from the way in which it was played. Thus, an oblique stroke represents the guiro part; vertical lines, the Indian jingles—each of which was played by one child holding it by one end and beating it on the palm of the other hand. The Indian rattle has a wiggly line for its shake; the form of the Cricket's symbol suggests the operation of the clicker. Numbered circles mark the chordal dulcimer's part, the number referring to the chord it plays. Each part was in a different color.

The score approaches conventional notation; when the players are to play twice as fast, the joining of the separate marks suggests eighth notes. It was placed on the floor in front of the seated players to be easily seen. Facing the players across the score, the leader directed with a pointer, marking the place of each successive beat of the music; whenever his pointer reached a child's part, she played. It gave the girls great satisfaction to use the score; the musical experience and success of their ensemble playing pleased them and gave them a feeling of pride.

There are many ways in which charts for instrumental playing can be made. The "Prayer of the Cricket" had its own symbols, which the girls quickly came to read. Such procedures can be used widely. Also effective are various forms of picture notation using representations of instruments or nonmusical objects, and on a higher level, color-coded musical notation. (*See Music for the Hearing Impaired — and Other Special Groups*, pages 112–116, 163, and 192–189, for details.)

Conclusion

The foregoing suggestions should not be taken as rigid directions for hard-and-fast technique. Conducting style should arise naturally out of a dedication to the musical activities and an enjoyment of the children's work. Inevitably, there is an element of *showmanship* in this work—the leader has to create, through the way she leads the group and conducts the players, a live, purposeful atmosphere that will foster the enriching experiences musical activities can give. These experiences must be clear, vital, and colorful if they are to involve the children deeply and to remain supportively in their memories. Not everything that is done for them can stay in their memories with such constructive associations. Through musical activities we endeavor to build in each child's memory an integration of achievement, positive self-experience, and social success that cannot fade but that becomes, if our therapeutic hopes are realized, a source of developmental strength in the child's life. Showmanship, therefore, is never used to entertain or merely excite the children, but to arouse their perceptive awareness and to lead them into participation with all the consciousness of which they are capable.

Chapter Four

Plays with Music

The development and performance of a play with handicapped children can be a dynamically stimulating event in the social life of a school or institution; its effects reach through the children, the staff, parents, and interested groups. The staging of the play—the rich experience of story, action, speech, song, music, color, and costume—can be an imposing achievement, the participation of the children impressive and heart-warming. When the play has been written and produced expressly for them, and depends upon their involvement for its realization, the performance transmits the children's capacities for care, perceptiveness, and cooperativeness; the audience experiences their commitment and sense of fulfillment. Pathology takes second place as the children's individualities are actively expressed.

Parents may be deeply thrilled and feel pride in their children and a closer connection to the teachers, particularly to those who produced the play. A play can often reveal undetected abilities, and it can be informative for staff members, who know the children under particular circumstances, to have the opportunity to see other aspects of their personalities.

For the children in the play, the performance is the consummation of a series of developing experiences. During the preceding weeks they have worked constructively with their teachers, enjoying and becoming familiar with the story, variously concentrating upon the action, practicing speech, and learning new songs. The sequence of musical and dramatic experiences has engaged them. With growing interest they have watched each other being active in their parts. Some have found freedom from forms of handicap and have possibly learned to use new capacities, others have developed some carefulness or confidence in self-expression. The play has grown and with it has grown their awareness of all it comprises; as its finished form evolved they felt satisfaction in the completeness this gave their participation. With the approach of the performance date they had the stimulation of being fitted with costumes and of wearing them in dress rehearsals.

These experiences bear the children into the performance. In the success of this occasion all the positive achievements of the rehearsals find social confirmation. The players feel pleasure in the warmth of the audience's interest; from being appreciated and applauded, needed feelings of self-esteem and self-assurance develop. There is satisfaction in being able to demonstrate abilities or sensitivities that are often obscured. They communicate something of themselves to parents and to the adult world. This is fulfilling.

The performance makes its impression on those children in the audience; they remember the songs, the colorfulness, the movements, speech, or parts of the action that intrigued them. At some level they will also remember the personal qualities the players put into their roles. All these experiences lay a foundation and set standards for work they may do in the future.

The realization of effective dramatic work with handicapped children depends to a great extent on the way music is used to support it. Comprehensive, vital experiences, which are not otherwise possible, can be created for all types of handicapped children when music is used to bring life and movement into a play, to give expression to its characters, atmosphere to the story, and structure to the action.

The Choice of Subjects for Plays

A story selected for a play should be appropriate—in maturity of content, emotionally, and in its forms of activity—for the children who are going to work on it. It should be capable of effecting their maximum engagement and of yielding satisfying, developmental experiences. The theme and events must also be practicable for adequate and effective staging in a small number of scenes that are not too complicated for the players.

With young children the aim will most often be to create a focus of stable, enjoyable experience and activity that will arouse and coordinate the responses of individuals and stimulate social interaction. Choose stories needing little dialogue that does not refer directly to action, and those with scope for varied, purposeful activity that could be like a game. Plots should be simple: a story that follows one character through a succession of events and encounters will provide a central role for a more able child; this can carry the main action and integrate several shorter, simpler parts for other children. Stories in which a number of characters enact similar forms of action or dialogue are also suitable for this group.

When working with somewhat more advanced children, plays may be richer in theme; the range of experience given through them should be wider and aim to foster the development of emotionally perceptive understanding. Within the structure of the dramatic action the characters and scenes can express qualities and feelings such as dignity, beauty, mystery, kindness, humor, foolishness, friendliness, sadness, loneliness, anger, wonder, etc., for children to portray and experience. The older educable and play-experienced trainable children will respond purposefully to serious dramatic presentations of idealism, sacrifice, loyalty, devotion, tenderness, courage, etc., personally sustained by characters in the play.

A large part of humanity's heritage of literature is available for dramatization into plays for handicapped children. From all over the world are folk tales and fables, mythologies, epics and legends, which have a universality in their imagery and content and a moral directness to which children respond. Religious poems and parables of many countries, the Old and New Testaments, contain inspiring, exemplifying themes. Stories may be taken from history, the biographies of famous men, and from suitable novels or tales of adventure.

The fact that in dramatizing any story you will be *working it out in action* widens the choice of possible subjects; many stories that children would find incomprehensible or overcomplex when told become meaningful and stimulating when developed into plays in which they participate. It does not matter if a child is unable to comprehend an entire play intellectually, provided that the part he plays has active sense for him in itself and in its connections with other characters in the action. The players experience the story's succession of events *from within*, and the significance of each child's role in the overall play becomes more perceptible to him as the action builds up in rehearsals.

Dramatization

The dramatizer of a story aims to realize its theme in a creative arrangement of speech, song, action, music, staging, and costume that will engage the children she is working with. The speech, action, and staging give the meaning of a play and its structure; songs, music, and costume give it expression, character, and life. These dramatic elements should be used freely to suit the capabilities of the children and the requirements of the story that has been chosen.

When working a story into a play a certain amount of trial and error will be involved in exploring and discovering its dramatic possibilities. Often parts of the play's structure will have to be built or evolved carefully to accommodate the children; at other times, out of the story itself, and in answer to the children's responses to it, spontaneous ideas for action, song, or speech will catch the essence of a scene and enliven it.

A practical and effective way of dramatizing a story for any particular group of children is to work on it experimentally with them. To illustrate how this can be done and what could happen, visualize making a play from the story of "The Musicians of Bremen" with a group of trainable or young educable children.

Commence work on it five or six weeks before the performance date, allowing three rehearsals weekly. Start to evolve the play in the classroom, clearing plenty of floor space for action. Begin simply by introducing the characters of the Miller and his Donkey. Choose two children to act these characters, giving them some identifying piece of costume or a prop—a white apron for the Miller, a pair of ears for the Donkey—to add interest. Put out a table to be the mill. Describe how the Donkey carried sacks of flour and have the Donkey carry sacks. When the Donkey becomes old it is harder for him to carry such heavy loads; act this out in a simple way with the children. Tell of and act out the Miller's impatience and his desire to get rid of the Donkey. Let the Miller go to sleep in his "mill" and the Donkey set out on his journey.

Set a table in another part of the room for the Hunter's house. Choose children to be the Hunter and his Dog, again with simple props to give them some characterization, a gun for the Hunter and a tail for the Dog. Describe how the Hunter went hunting, how his Dog caught every bird he shot and brought it to him. Act this out with the children, perhaps with a small bundle of cloth for a bird. The Dog becomes old, he cannot always find the bird; he has lost his teeth and is unable to carry the bird without dropping it. This is acted, too. The Hunter becomes angry and says that the Dog has to go. When the Donkey and the sad Dog meet they go off together to "make music in Bremen."

This may be as far into the story as one can get in the first period spent on it, perhaps not even this far. In the succeeding sessions repeat what has been done and go on to introduce the Cat and the Rooster in the same way.

During these first two or three sessions the children's participation may be sketchy—some children may be confused. But as the story is repeated and the characters and their interrelationships are established, the order and action will become clearer to them. In these repetitions gradually crystallize the speech lines; they should be simple, short, and direct, with only essential words. For example, such a line as "I'm going to get rid of that Donkey!" can become part of the play and repeated for the Dog, Cat, and Rooster.

Do not drill the children to speak the lines, particularly if they have pronounced speech handicaps. Encourage by example, repeating the lines yourself as often as necessary so that they are heard distinctly and with inflection. The play should not be labored but led, out of the situation and in response to what the children can do, toward a dramatically concise form. At this point songs may be evolved to carry some of the speech lines and action; their words may be taken directly from the simple speech you have been using. The meeting between the Donkey and the Dog might go as follows:

Donkey: (*speaking*): "What's the matter? You look sad!"

Dog (or everyone) *sings:* "Old and Sad"

Donkey (*speaking*): "Can you bark?"

Dog barks feebly.

Donkey (*speaking*): "Good, louder!"

Dog barks with a little more strength.

Donkey (*speaking*) : *"Like this!" He brays.*

Dog barks loudly.

Donkey (or everyone) *sings:* "To Bremen"

The song is repeated if necessary as the Donkey and Dog march off together. They stand or sit to one side while the Cat is introduced into the play. Then both come into the scene and meet her; the dialogue and songs take the same form as before.

The action is the same with the Rooster. The march becomes the theme song of this part of the story; when all four animals go off together, a new chorus may be added to form the climax of this section such as:

Bray don- key! (Donkey brays) Bark, dog! (Dog barks). Meaou, cat!, (Cat meaous).

Crow, roos - ter! (Rooster crows). We'll make mus-ic in Bre-men! (They all bray, bark, meou and crow)

We'll make mus-ic in Bre - men!

They march around the classroom.

Go on to the next scene by introducing the tree where the four characters plan to spend the night. The tree may be improvised by using a small table; the Donkey and the Dog sit beside it on the floor, the Cat lies on it, while the Rooster, who is to be in the topmost branches, stands on it. (As a class project, a tree may be made from cardboard, colored, and fastened to the table.) As the characters settle in and around the tree there can be music. Resonator bells might be effective in this scene.

While the four animals are at the tree, describe the Robbers' house; set up another table with make-believe, marvelous things to eat and drink on it. Possibly be a Robber yourself and have three or four children come to eat with you. Play-act having a wonderful feast with them—great eating games can be played with paper cups, and with pies, cakes, etc., improvised from cardboard boxes and blackboard erasers. When this scene is established bring the animals into the action. The Rooster sees the light that shines from the Robbers' house. All the animals come to look through the window at the feast. They say how hungry they are. The Donkey gets an idea: the Dog is to stand on his back, the Cat on the Dog's back, and the Rooster on the back of the Cat. They are all to make their sounds together as they jump through the window to scare the Robbers away. This cannot be acted, but something striking and dramatic has to be done here. One possibility is to have the Donkey crouch; beside him—the far side from an audience's viewpoint —stands the Dog; beside the Dog the Cat stands on a chair; beside the Cat the Rooster on a taller chair, stool or a table. From these positions they jump forward braying, barking, miaowing, and crowing together. The Robbers flee; the heroes sit at the table and enjoy the food. (This piece of action can become a popular game.)

Go over this scene in sequence with the previous one, again developing simple phrases for the children that carry the story, while evolving the short lines you will use as narrator to sustain the action in the finished play. During this time you may be gaining some idea of which children will be taking parts in the performance.

By now, the play will probably be in its third week and the children sufficiently familiar with the story for rehearsals to begin in the auditorium. Using the facilities of stage and auditorium for the movement of characters and for the arranging of scenes, work to form the play for performance. Because the main action takes place inside the Robbers' house, this interior scene must be set on the stage (with chairs around a large table laden with food; there is also a fireplace). It is hidden by the curtain during the earlier action, which must take place on the stage in front of the curtain or on the auditorium floor. The tree must be in the auditorium, over to one side; during rehearsals it may, for example, be built around a stepladder.

As the positions for the action are determined, the need for music and the parts it can play become increasingly apparent. When music accompanies the players as they go from one scene to another, interest and continuity are maintained; when a song tells about the action in a scene the whole experience acquires a memorable character; children are drawn into the play as they sing it.

The combination of action, music, and speech in this middle section of the story may possibly evolve in this way: following the music to which the characters settle at the tree, there is a short pause. The curtain opens on the feasting Robbers. No speech is heard as they eat and pass food to each other but descriptive music sets the mood—there is something mysterious about them.

After the Feasting Song, the Robbers' Music continues; the four animals put their heads together. The narrator tells the Donkey's idea; as he describes it the animals take up their positions. Music builds up the expectation, and on a musical cue they burst into the room (a cymbal crash can heighten the shock). The Robbers give a shout, jump up, and run from the stage; now the animals sit at the table and begin to eat.

When they have finished, they find their places to sleep.

The third part of the story, in which a Robber is sent back to reconnoiter and is so severely frightened that all the Robbers leave the country forever—and their house to the four animals, is worked out in the same experimental way, its form evolving as the staging is determined and the music incorporated. The play should close with a song, perhaps in this style:

Happily (♩ = 80)

This is just the right house for a don - key and a dog, for a
just the right size for a don - key and a dog, for a

roos - ter and a cat, This is just the right house. It is
roos - ter and a cat. It is

[2.] just the right size. They will nev - er go a - way, not the

don - key, not the dog, not the roos - ter, not the cat, They will

161

nev - er go a - way. It will be a hap - py house for a don - key and a dog, for a roos - ter and a cat, It will be a hap-py house. It will be a hap-py house. It will be a hap-py house.

During the last two weeks of rehearsal, the final choice of cast will be made. It does not matter if children who want to take parts do not speak distinctly; in a play of this kind the narrator can repeat lines after the children whenever necessary for an audience. Costumes should be made and fitted during this time.

The children are not *told* the story, they *experience* it as a many-sided activity that develops with and through their involvement to become a complete musical-dramatic structure. When all the facets of such a play and all the details of its action are created with the children's participation in mind, and connected meaningfully for them to lead the action forward, surprisingly large dramatic structures can be evolved in which they can function with confidence and perception.

This method of dramatization is applicable in working with almost all trainable children, and with at least the elementary grades of educable children. "The Musicians of Bremen" illustrates a simple, active play for 12 or 14 characters, appropriate for trainable children up to 13 or so and for the educable up to grade 3. With children two or three years older a wide range of stories, of which "Dummling and the Golden Goose," "The Water of Life" (Grimm's Fairy Tales), "The Magic Herdboy" (an African story), and "No-So-What" (a Finnish folktale) are representative examples, can be dramatized in the same way. Their richer imagery and content call for a greater variety in speech and action, and their range of dramatic experience stimulates a more receptive, more thoughtfully feeling response.

For older and more capable children, play-experienced or high grade trainable of 15 years or more, or educable of 12 and up, the dramatizing of a more complex or emotionally intense story will probably have to be done with less improvisation. Initially, the main action of a scene may be introduced experimentally to the children to prepare them and to assess their dramatic potentials relative to it, but the seriousness of the subject and the need to convey the content through means technically within the children's abilities call for more careful writing and planning than are possible while working in the classroom. The lines and action of each scene will have to be prepared beforehand and then presented to the children flexibly. As you work with them on the scene, any changes necessary to render the parts more suitable for the players or to increase the play's dramatic strength should be made; often a player's spontaneous response or rewording of a line improves the action.

The dramatic work on one scene in the classroom can be a guide to the writing of the next, and thus center the whole building of the play upon the children's involvement.

In the dramatization of all plays for handicapped children, the principles of using speech, music, and action illustrated in "The Musicians of Bremen" apply. Defined separately they are:

Use direct speech that is simple, natural, and appropriate to the children.

Interrelate the speech lines of different characters so that one line invites or supports the next.

Repeat forms of dialogue and action to develop a scene.

Alternate speech lines with musical phrases to give timing and mood to the children's speaking.

Give character to a person or scene with a song; the words should be appropriate, descriptive, and expressively set.

Build the action with repetitions of songs, using different verses when necessary for different characters or situations.

Set the mood of action or a scene with music.

Allow plenty of room for action and create opportunities for players to move or march through the space available, usually to music or a song.

Dramatize a scene to have a high point or climax to focus the action and increase interest.

Separate scenes spatially to make them distinct.

Use these principles selectively to suit the play and carefully to support the children's participation, and they will create a limitless diversity of dramatic experience.

Play production can also be enriched by:

Creating contrasts between scenes in mood, pace of action, music, etc.

Intensifying the action with a speech chorus where this is suitable to a play, especially in work with older children. Dramatic situations can be heightened when a speech chorus interjects revealing or forceful comments upon the action. The chorus may describe important events that cannot be acted; it may link scenes by narrating events that cannot be shown, or describe the passing of time or changes in the development of the characters' roles. It may counsel or warn actors, or encourage a character who is to attempt a difficult feat. The chorus may speak at any appropriate time during the play and be closely knit into the dramatic structure. It may speak only before and after scenes, thus providing a "frame" for the actors and the drama. Five to ten speakers make a good, cohesive working group. Usually they say their lines in unison; single voices may be used for contrast. Lines can be free in rhythmic flow or based on a definitely accented rhythm; they may rhyme. A speech chorus can be eloquent and powerful when combined with music.

Beginning and ending plays with processions of the cast. An inviting opening and a rounded quality of completion may be given to a play by processions of the cast. To an opening song

164

or music the players enter from the rear of the auditorium and walk in procession through the audience. This is the occasion for parents, relatives, and friends to enjoy the children in their costumes; young children have the opportunity to become accustomed to the audience and find their parents and friends while stepping into the action with musical support. Through the color, character, and variety of their costumes, and the spirit of the processional music, the mood with which the play begins is set. The order of the characters in the procession should be appropriate to the parts they play. The procession will take them to the places they must occupy when the play begins; it may make something of a circuit of the audience. This will depend upon the size of the auditorium, the number in the cast, and the nature of the play. When the play has ended, usually after the applause, a closing procession takes the entire cast through the audience again and out of the auditorium.

Means of dramatization more specifically concerned with music, staging, and costume are given in the following sections.

Dramatization Through Music

Music composed or arranged to be performed with a play must express, in its overall quality, the general character and mood of the play. Although the music will need to be varied to depict, foreshadow, or emphasize the events that take place, a unity of mood should be maintained. If you plan to use music already composed, there are many fine collections of folk music of different countries and excellent collections of spirituals among which you may well find the particular music you need. Feel free to use the music of a beautiful folk song or spiritual without the words, but be careful to choose one that is relatively unfamiliar so that it will not have associations incongruous to the story.

Other possibilities for music are the simple instrumental pieces composed by Bach, Schumann, Beethoven, Mozart, Ravel, and others. The great variety of character and mood available in each composer's work provides wide selection from which to choose the music most suitable for your purposes.

The choosing of the places in the play where music will

be most effective is a vital part of the musical planning. Introductory music in the form of an overture or a song may be desirable; music before a scene, or between scenes as connecting links, can be highly effective; when it accompanies the dramatic action, a climax, or emotionally charged lines, music intensifies the experience; it can be fitting for the close of a play. Some balance between the amount of music and the action of the play will be necessary—this can be determined by experiment— for too much music will obscure the story and detract from the importance of the actors' roles, too little may make the play seem unsubstantial, even incomplete.

When the introductory music accompanies a procession of the actors, it may be thought of as a description of the characters in the procession, as a musical expression of the mood of the opening scene, or as depicting a dramatic event in which the actors will be involved. Such musical foreshadowing will give the event an added force when it occurs. The quality of mood of the processional music or song adds character to a play when it reflects its content. Jubilant music or buoyant, outgoing songs will be descriptive of some plays; for others, music with inwardness, wonder perhaps, or mystery will be suitable. At the beginning of "The Children's Christmas Play" the players enter to the thoughtful, calm, yet expectant feeling of "O Come All Ye Faithful." The closing procession to "Hark the Herald Angels Sing" carries more of the quality of affirmation, warm celebration.

All the examples of musical dramatization in this section are taken from "The Story of Artaban,*" a serious play for children in their teens. The general content of a play can be depicted in a processional song. In this play it is sung by a solo voice.

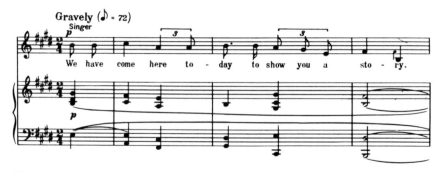

The sto-ry of Ar-ta-ban, the sto-ry of the

long, long jour-ney, the long, long jour-ney of Ar-ta-ban.

Music used to open a scene should be just long enough to set the mood and arouse anticipation. The procession takes the players to their places on the stage. The song is immediately followed by music which quickly builds to a climax—Artaban's opening line. A drum and cymbal play with the piano. The percussion is played by one child.

Example:

Artaban stands and looks at the sky. He searches among the stars. The Angel walks slowly forward, stands behind Artaban and raises his arm, pointing stage left to the sky.

Very slowly (♩ = 40)

ARTABAN *(Pointing to the sky.)*
There! There it is! There is the new star!

When music connects scenes, or forms an interlude during scene or costume changes, it can begin in the mood of the scene that has just ended and then be modified, varied, or completely changed, to create the mood of the scene to come. It may be written to indicate, through previous character identification with specific music, a character who is to appear.

In the following example, music introduces a new scene. Changes of costume and props are made while it is played and sung. It is quiet, gentle, expressing the action with which the scene begins.

Example:

Songs may be composed or chosen to lend their special qualities to the musical-dramatic structure. They can establish mood and effect abrupt changes of mood. They also further the action of the play by arousing feelings of suspense or anticipation. Songs are an appealing vehicle for the expression of a character's emotions; these, set to music, may reveal a deeper aspect of his personality.

This illustration below is the song sung by Artaban that expresses his feelings about the star he has just seen, for which he has waited so long.

168

Example:

None of the music during the play should slow down or impede the ongoing dramatic movement. This is particularly true when short musical statements are used to enhance brief moments of dramatic intensity. Here, any instrumental sounds must be true to the situation they accompany, the melodic lines clear and telling, the harmonies expressive, the rhythmic element precise. The music can begin slightly before or with the line, movement, or gesture it accompanies, and end with or shortly after it, or the music may begin and end before the dramatic happening. In such places the music should never overpower the acting or the actors' voices. If a loud dynamic is essential for expressive purposes, cut off the music just before the lines are to be spoken to ensure that they will be clearly heard.

The tragic climax of "The Story of Artaban" is heightened by music. *Example:*

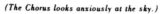
(The Chorus looks anxiously at the sky.)

(All except the Angel, Artaban and the Captives fall to their knees.)

Speech Chorus

Thun-der!   Light-ning!   The earth is shak-ing!

(They shield their heads)   *(They surround Artaban, appealing to him, imploring him.)*

Sp.C.

Hous - es are fal-ling!   Save us!   Save us!   Save us!

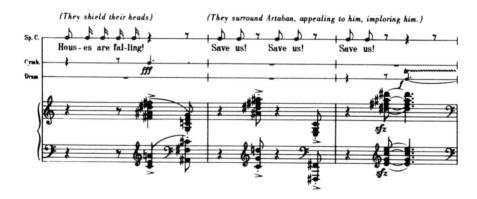

170

The combination of a speech chorus and music can be highly exciting; the voices of the children are able to equal the volume of the music and with it achieve a stirring climax. When the speech chorus, as it narrates an event in the play, is accompanied by music, the words can be spoken in a definite expressive rhythm supported by the same rhythm in the music. This technique is stimulating for the speakers and dramatically impressive for the audience.

Example:

A solo adult voice, used as part of the musical conception, provides possibilities for expressing a complex narrative beyond the children's capacities. The singer can carry the thread of a description or statement, the children adding essential spoken lines to the phrases she sings.

Searching in Egypt for thirty-three years, Artaban meets all manner of people in difficulties and helps them. This is vitally important to the story but cannot be acted, and for a narrator to describe it would be dramatically flat at this point in the play. The question of how best to convey it was solved by writing the Interlude in which the seven players on stage (four were offstage changing for the next scene) were variously given very short, simple narrative lines to speak—which were answered, connected, and led forward by lines given to the singer. In the antiphonal dialogue between speakers and singer—structured and given expressive power by the music—the story of the thirty-three years is told.

MERCHANT

(He steps forward and stands between the 1st Soldier and the Woman.)

He looked in cities.

WOMAN

(Standing where she is.)

In villages.

CAPTAIN

(He steps forward and stands between the 2nd Soldier and the Mother.)

In palaces.

ABGARUS

(He steps forward and stands, in the center of the stage between the Woman and the Mother.)

In churches.

He searched for thir - ty-three years but did not find

Him.

1st SOLDIER He helped them.

He found poor peo - ple.___

2nd SOLDIER He made them well.

He found sick peo - ple.___

He found hun - gry peo - ple.___

CAPTAIN He fed them.

MOTHER He gave them water.

He found thirst - y peo - ple.___

173

The seriousness of teen-aged players and their total commitment to their roles are expressed in this closing scene of "The Story of Artaban." Dramatic effect is often achieved most directly through simplicity in set and costumes when music creates the mood.

175

Instrumental Parts for Children in the Play's Music

The music for a play may include instrumental parts to be played by children. A single child playing instruments essential to the character of the music, or an orchestra of perhaps six or even more children, can provide a variety of descriptive effects in tone and timbre that can be used expressively to deepen any dramatic experience. The number of players will be determined to some extent by the number of instruments you feel necessary for the musical support of the dramatic content of the play.

Select those instruments you feel to be expressive of the story and its characters and try them out with these in mind. Think of the instruments as "musical characters," each to contribute its individual effect to the whole. Make experiments with dynamics and with various tonal combinations to explore their musical-dramatic possibilities. Blow a horn softly, sustaining the tone; make a great crash with the hand cymbals; give a single, soft stroke on the gong and follow it with a still softer one on the cymbal; choose pairs of resonator bells that will sound different intervals—C′ and F#′, B′ C″, C′ G′, D′ - C#″, etc.—and play them many times successively and together; blow two horns of different pitches with a ringing forte. Such experimentation can be helpful and even inspiring when you set about choosing instruments and the places in the score where they will be able to make their most telling effects.

The sounds of various instruments can be highly suggestive in delineating characters: a gong may accompany the entrance of a magician or some other mysterious figure; a zither may evoke the gentle quality of the princess, a horn depict the personality of a hunter, a challenger, or announce the arrival of an important personage.

Use the instruments experimentally with the children. You may find that in practice some instruments will have to be eliminated and others substituted because they prove to be not directly expressive of the story, incompatible with the music or the play's action as it develops, or unsuitable for the children. All the instruments used must be capable of engaging and challenging the players, while giving them stimulating musical experiences.

In order that the players will derive the greatest benefit from their participation, have in mind as you write the music for the instruments what each child is able to do, what he might achieve, and what you would like to see him accomplish through the experiences he will be receiving. This will guide you in the degree of technical difficulty and expressive demand you write into each part.

The music you play yourself—on the piano, guitar, auto-harp, or whatever your instrument might be—will unify the parts the children play. It will support their playing rhythmically, melodically, and harmonically, and create the structure necessary for conveying a total musical experience. Your music should enhance and bring out each individual instrumental or vocal part to increase its effectiveness. Unless some dramatic moment in the play calls for a big musical effect to be achieved only by technically difficult music, your part should always be proportionate to the children's parts in complexity and forcefulness.

The music of an overture can be composed or arranged in such a way that each instrument has an opportunity to play a brief solo part. This will alert the instrumentalists, stimulate them, bring them into the play, and give them a feeling of their musical responsibilities from the start.

In the Overture to "The Children's Christmas Play" the various instruments play their solo parts in three well-defined sections; in each one the music changes to support and enhance the contrasting qualities of the instruments' sounds. None of this music is repeated later; it suggests the events to come and prepares the mood for the play.

178

In this play music accompanies the entrances of each group of characters to give an impression of the quality of their dramatic presence in the story. The types of instruments the children play are an essential part of this depiction of character. The King's music possesses a certain barbaric splendor and dignity.

The orchestra is playing the overture of "The Children's Christmas Play" for a dress rehearsal. The children play together on the final chords. Three bell players look toward the stage, enthralled by the barn scene and the animal costumes; others respond to the sounds they create or to the character of their instruments.

School District of Philadelphia

181

The Shepherd's music has a pastoral quality.

Example:

Small bells give warmth and gentleness to Mary's and Joseph's music.

(See page 112)

It is advisable not to use the entire orchestra too often. Save the ensemble, the tutti, for an especially dramatic place or for times when its musical effect will be most suitable. Compose or arrange all the music to create tonal variety, use each instrument so that it will be most expressively effective whenever it is played. In this way no instrument will lose its impact through over use and no child will be overtaxed by his part.

Rehearsing the Play

Working with the Cast
When you first begin to develop a story into a new play, you can have no idea how the project will turn out. Work empirically, exploring the story's possibilities for the children's experience and activity. Be faithful to the story, treat its characters and events objectively yet imaginatively. Use your own words to present it, freely expressing in simple phrases and with illustrating actions any complex concepts. Be prepared with the materials you will need and improvise anything a situation might require.

Working with an already written play calls for much the same attitude, because when you first introduce it you cannot foresee all the effects and experiences which your class and you may attain. There are several ways of rehearsing a written play: one is to teach its songs first and then build the action around them; another, more preferable, is to recreate the play as if it were being dramatized experimentally, evoking the children's interest by working freely with the scenes and leading their involvement toward the scripted form—the words of the speech and the songs being prefigured as you rehearse and gradually made definite. A third way, with educable children, is to give the players suitably prepared copies of the script, letting them learn their lines and improve enunciation, etc., as part of school work or speech therapy, and rehearse the play conventionally.

The extent to which a play will be authentically *acted* depends upon the ages and abilities of the players. Educable children or individuals with a natural flair for acting can commit themselves to a genuine dramatic portrayal of their roles; trainable or young children will live more immediately in their own responses to the whole play experience.

In the rehearsals you will be working with each child's responsive interest as this comes through the developmental condition of his particular personality. Individual limitations in verbal or vocal expression, perception, comprehension, behavioral control—or maladjustment, emotional disturbance or physical handicap, etc.—will come to expression and should always be worked with positively. When a child's difficulties manifest themselves in a particular situation in a play, work encouragingly to lead him so that he can go through his part in a scene and experience something of it regardless of his handicap. In succeeding rehearsals try to make the overall experience of building the play important and engaging enough to inspire motivation for progressive effort; maintain its stability so that in repetitions of the structured activity of the child's part he can achieve development. Any freedom or capability a child realizes in a scene becomes part of that scene's action, and so has social as well as personal significance for him. This can be effective therapy.

With educable children work on the inflection and volume of speech, on timing, body movement, and gesture, both with individual players and in the coordinated activity of the group. Show trainable or young children how to move as befits their part or action, how to walk with dignity, how to move slowly or sadly, how to go on tiptoe, and the like. By demonstration encourage them to make telling gestures expressively. Work to make their speech as appropriate as is reasonably possible to a situation. Do all this to increase the children's consciousness of the play and to make it possible for them to realize— through their inner experiences of the movements and gestures they make—the emotional qualities of scenes and action. It will often be necessary to get into the action yourself to lead the children through a scene; evoke its mood, be as dramatic or gentle as a situation requires, and tell things about the characters to make them live.

When a child's speech is blurred, too fast, or fragmentary, it can be strengthened and formed by fitting important words to expressive actions, or by practicing lines to specially prepared or improvised music which supports them in rhythm, inflection, and emotional quality.

Rehearse scenes that place challenging demands upon players as many times and as carefully as needed. Give individual instruction. Older children may be stimulated when part of the cast is called for special rehearsals to go over particular scenes in some detail.

Working with the Instrumental Players

At the first orchestral rehearsal give each child a turn to play each instrument so that he can handle it, experience its tone quality, and perceive the way the tone is produced. This will arouse all the children's interest and become a preparation for the musical unity they can develop and experience as members of the orchestra. When the instruments are presented with care and with respect for their musical possibilities, the children will feel that they are important and special. This will become part of their attitude when they play their parts.

When you introduce the instrumental parts into rehearsal, try experimenting with them with different children. If necessary, support their playing with your instrument even though the music may not call for this when the parts are learned. Playful musical give-and-take with the parts between you and the players can be an excellent means of establishing and fixing them in the children's memories.

At first, some children's playing may be uncertain or insecure; encourage and lead them until they find the rhythm, the tempo, or the placement and can play an approximation of how their parts should sound.

It is well to repeat each section, or part of a section, as many times as the children can do so whenever this is necessary. Through repetitions in which the players really work, their playing will improve, and they will feel their parts in the ensemble and come to grasp the meaning and character of the music. Although perfection in performance may not always be attainable because of the nature of a child's handicap, the best possible should be the goal of rehearsals.

When the orchestra is composed of less handicapped children, who will be able to learn to play their parts without special preparation, work on the music in its sequence in the score. These children will be interested in the musical-dramatic continuity of their parts; the relationship of the music they make to the story and its action will be important to them.

An orchestra of more than three or four players should first achieve some degree of musical competence before a rehearsal is arranged with the actors. When the players are fairly secure in their parts they will be able to take the stimulating experiences of the play and not be overwhelmed by their first encounter with all its dramatic activities. However, when the music is closely woven into the play and is integral to its structure, joint rehearsals will have to be conducted from the beginning.

Dress rehearsals are exciting events. It may be wise to have several so that the orchestra members will become accustomed to seeing their schoolmates dressed in costume. These rehearsals can also be important for the children in the cast, enabling them to become completely at ease with the music and to feel more deeply its essential relationship to their roles and to the play. If the audience is to consist of trainable or young children, invite them to at least one dress rehearsal to prepare them for the performance.

Staging the Scenes and Action

The sequence of speech, music, and action organize the children's experience of the play in time; the definite arrangement of the scenes and of the movement of the action give it an organization in space. Experiment to find the most effective way of using whatever staging facilities are available. The size and shape of the stage, the amount of space (if any) on the apron before the curtain, the ways of entering and leaving the stage, the connections between it and the auditorium, the amount of room on the auditorium floor in front of the first row of seats, the size of the auditorium, the position of the aisles and exits all hold possibilities for staging that can make the production engaging for both the players and the audience.

Stage a play with effective simplicity. If the auditorium at your disposal has a well-equipped stage avoid using any unnecessary technical apparatus or stagecraft; these can interfere with the actors' experience of the play and weaken the contact between them and the audience, particularly if the players are young. When there is an apron in front of the curtain, it is often better with young children to stage the play here and on the auditorium floor; if required, the stage itself may be kept for an important interior setting or a special scene. For older children who can act with more dramatic awareness, use the technical possibilities of the stage effectively and sparingly.

If the facilities available are limited to the floor of a gymnasium or sash-connected classrooms, this need be no deterrent; improvise whatever will serve the action simply, using platforms, screens, benches, and other classroom furniture; the players' costumes and the music will create the dramatic atmosphere.

Many plays may be staged by seating the players in a semicircle, open toward the audience, around the acting area. This may be on stage, on the apron, or on the auditorium floor, as the play requires. The cast remains here throughout most of the play; individual players step forward to enter the action and return to their seats between their parts. At times players may exit through the auditorium or stage wings if the action or later entrances require it. This kind of arrangement, especially suitable for plays in which the story centers upon the action of one or two leading characters, gives an easy, intimate coordination to young children's playing; it can create a dignified mood and focus of dramatic intensity in plays with older children. This semicircle of supporting players may also take the role of a speech chorus. As all scenes are imaginary, no stage set is needed other than the general setting in which the play takes place; this may consist of flats or curtains.

When sets and stage properties are being used, their design and color should be in keeping with the content of the play. They can be uncomplicated in construction: boats, trees, palaces, and the like can be made from cut-outs nailed onto supporting frames. Much can be done with large pieces of variously colored material: green or earth-colored cloth thrown over a structure of tables creates a cave; a chair covered with red or gold material becomes a throne; appropriately colored materials draped over painting easels can make a house.

Few plays for young children will require any special lighting; a warm natural light will generally suffice, especially if the background curtains are warmly colored. The players should be clearly visible at all times. For most of these plays the auditorium should not be blacked out, any action that takes place in it being lit by daylight or by the standard lighting fixtures. More serious plays will usually need the auditorium darkened.

Lighting changes should be made only when they are essential to the action; they may be coordinated with the music or the speech chorus. On stages without means for dimming lights and changing colors smoothly, no changes should be made unless they can be done with the curtain closed and between scenes, except in rare dramatic situations that require a startling change.

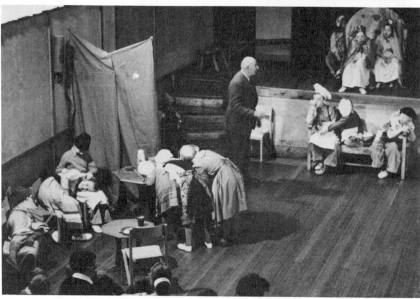

Scenes from two plays given at Sunfield Children's Homes. Those on the left are from a production of "Dummling and the Golden Goose." In the upper picture Dummling shares his bottle of sour wine with the Old Grey Man—it becomes sweet as he does so. In the lower picture Dummling (far left) sleeps in the Inn; the Golden Goose is on the table. The three daughters of the Innkeeper, who have come to take feathers from it, are now stuck to each other and must "spend the night with the goose." The narrator leads the story on. The King, seated on the apron of the stage, is absorbed by the action.

In the finale of "The Windmill Play" one of the folk dances the children have learned is used to give a gay, yet formal ending.

Costumes

When the time comes for costume fitting, the children's experience of play-making is quickened. The costumes make a big impression; their colorfulness, their style and texture, the utter difference between them and everyday clothes, and the novelty of being fitted and seeing how they all look thrill and stimulate the players.

All that has been developed in speech, music, and action takes on a new dimension of color and appearance. Each role acquires its visual identity for the children; from seeing the entire cast in costume they experience something of a tableau or image of the play. Costumes turn the play into an event! Each child's costume makes his own part a stronger reality for him and increases his sense of participating in an important happening. The players, united by their costumes, become a special group with a particular purpose. The attentiveness and care of the teachers who fit and dress the players heighten the significance of these experiences.

For most kinds of plays for handicapped children the following styles of costumes are suggested: boys—smocks of various lengths and slip-on or button-up tunics, belted and loose, worn over the child's own pants in most cases, or with leggings; aprons for craftsmen; robes, capes, and scarves for dignitaries. Girls—smocks, pinafores, dresses, gowns, shawls, mantles, stoles, aprons, capes, etc. All can be in a variety of solid colors and suitable stripes or patterns. Hats, hoods, burnooses, jewelry, etc., and shoes, pumps, or sandals are worn as appropriate.

The basic materials for many costumes can often be obtained through appeals to parents or interested local groups. With some dyeing, creative cutting, and sewing, old bed linen, bed spreads, towels, burlap, curtains, upholstering materials, unwanted blouses, shirts, dresses, skirts, coats, and other items of clothing can be converted into excellent costumes. Discarded hats often need only the trimmings removed and some reshaping to be usable in a play. Costume jewelry is a welcome donation.

Costumes should be cut and sewn with functional simplicity and some leeway in size; all fitting and fastening can be done with safety pins. Drawstrings and belts also help in fitting.

Crowns, helmets, armor, and the like, may be cut out from gold or silver paper, pasted on buckram, lined with felt where necessary, and pinned or stapled to size. Or, the buckram may be sprayed the required color.

Hand properties such as tools for workmen and weapons for huntsmen or soldiers should be lightly but strongly made. (Not every object a player uses in a play need be represented, only those important for the action or for the child's experience; others should be suggested by the acting.)

Animal masks used should be lightweight. Most of those commercially available are too caricatured and their glossy surfaces inappropriate. They can, however, serve as foundations for more expressive masks. Paste thin felt or a similar material over a mask of this kind to obtain a better texture, then repaint it to portray something of the animal's real nature. Usually a mask will have to be fitted so that the player wears it above his head and not in front of his face. Often an animal part may be dressed by using, instead of a mask, a costume that suggests pertinent features, such as a cat's paws and whiskers, an elephant's ears and trunk.

Dressing a play is as creative as any other aspect of its production; the quality of each costume brings out the character of each part and adds to the overall effect of the play. Plays for younger children should be dressed simply, although some parts will call naturally for more ornate costumes than others. With older children, costumes can be appropriately elaborate in keeping with the style of production.

Performance

Try to carry the performance off with style. Have every technical detail of the production worked out and taken care of. Any teachers who are to assist by guiding the players at some point— changing costumes, preparing scenes, etc.—should have their functions clearly outlined and have practiced them. All assistance from the adults should go smoothly and be self-effacing; the play must have maximum operational support.

In many plays, particularly with younger children, the leader will be directly active, narrating and guiding the action so as to make all that the children do prominent, while maintaining the unity of the story. She will not be onstage in plays that use the stage, unless a special form of production is planned, but will support the players from a seat on the front row or a stool on the auditorium floor. The amount of narration she gives will depend on the dramatization—it should always be as little as possible; in some plays with older children there may be none. If there is an orchestra, the leader may also direct it when necessary.

Programs for the audience, with the players' and orchestra members' names, add to the occasion and often become treasured souvenirs. When the words of songs the audience is to sing cannot be picked up easily from repetitions in the play, give them out with the programs.

Chapter Five

Pif-Paf-Poltrie

"Fair Katrinelje and Pif-Paf-Poltrie" is one of the lesser-known folktales collected by the Brothers Grimm. It was first suggested as a story motif for a "therapeutic game" for moderately and severely retarded children by Herbert Geuter, M.D., Research Consultant, Sunfield Children's Homes, Worcestershire, England, in the spring of 1959. During October and November, 1959, the story was developed into a "working game" by the authors in their empirical work with several groups of English trainable children at the Sunfield Children's Homes. It was subsequently used for demonstration purposes with various groups of handicapped children in fourteen institutes in Great Britain and Europe. Following these demonstrations "Pif-Paf-Poltrie," as the game was now entitled, was tranlated into Danish, Dutch, and German.

The original English version of "Pif-Paf-Poltrie" was published by the Theodore Presser Co., Bryn Mawr, Pennsylvania, in 1961, a few months after the authors had begun to use the game in music therapy projects at the Devereux Schools, Devon, Pennsylvania, and the Department of Child Psychiatry, School of Medicine, University of Pennsylvania. The complete form of the game as it now appeared in the published copy was found to work as effectively with children here as it had with those for whom it had been developed in England. The same type of impact was made, an identical working spirit arose, and the same kinds of responses and results were seen.

As it was used repeatedly during the five years that followed, mostly at the Institute of Logopedics, Wichita, Kansas, and in the public schools of Philadelphia, changes occurred in details of the original dialogue and action. Some were made by the authors to suit the general needs and circumstances of the groups they worked with, others came from the children and would occur when a child's spontaneous response at a particular moment of the game was so true to the situation that it was incorporated from that time onward. None of these modifications altered its essential structure. Theodore Presser Company has published a revised edition of "Pif-Paf-Poltrie" that includes these changes. The directions given here are applicable to either edition.

As a working game the story of Pif-Paf-Poltrie creates a group activity that is both stimulating and integrating. It is eminently suitable for trainable children up to the age of 14 and older, and the primary grades of the educable. It is also suitable for regular kindergarten. Depending upon the children, it takes from 30 to 50 minutes to enact.

The size of the group can vary widely; the smallest number that can create the game is six; the authors have worked with groups as large as 50. As a general rule, younger children or those new to school life will benefit most in groups limited to about 10 or 12. It will work well with 9- to 13-year-olds in groups of 20, and 30 is possible if conditions require it. Much will depend upon the characteristic mood of the school or center, the relationship the children have to their teachers, and the spirit with which the game is led.

"Pif-Paf-Poltrie" will yield its best results when it is repeated each or every other week with a group. A consistency of approach, maintained from session to session, will keep its experience stable and progressive.

Descriptive Outline of "Pif-Paf-Poltrie"*

The children are seated in a semicircle around a large, clear floor space. The leader begins the game. She takes up a basket or box of leaves and strews them over the middle of the floor. She then takes the besom—a simple broom made of broomcorn or birch twigs bound to a stick (pronounced bee-zum)—unties the

---

*Copyright 1961 by Theodore Presser Co.
Copyright 1969 by Theodore Presser Co. All quotations used by permission.

knot, unbinds the pieces of broomcorn or twigs, and scatters them over the mess of leaves. She places the stick and the string in fairly obvious places in the room.

While making the mess the leader stimulates the children to comment upon it and leads their thinking toward the idea of cleaning it up. She asks for a volunteer to be Pif-Paf-Poltrie, who will "sweep it all clean." He comes into the center and Pif-Paf's special hat is placed on his head.

In the game Pif-Paf is looking for a wife—Fair Katie. The leader chooses her, she is given wrist bells to wear, and returns to her seat. A boy is chosen to be her father—Father Hollyberry; he stands in a cleared space in the middle of the mess, while Pif-Paf stands to one side. Everyone is quiet during the "Introductory Music." The leader speaks the opening words. These lead directly into "Pif-Paf-Poltrie's March." Pif marches around the mess. Father Hollyberry holds a make-believe sack of seeds under his arm and makes the motions of sowing wheat while the children sing:

If he wants to have Fair Katie,
    He must ask the way.
Where is Father Hollyberry?
    Here he is, good day!

As the March finishes, Pif stops before Father Hollyberry, raises his hat, and bows. They shake hands. Pif asks if he may marry Fair Katie. (During the dialogue, the leader directs or prompts as necessary.) He is told "Yes!" but also that he must ask Mother Milk-the-Cow, Brother High-and-Mighty, and Dear Old Sister Green-Cheese; and "If they all say 'yes,' Fair Katie is yours!" Pif asks for Mother Milk-the-Cow; a girl is chosen and kneels in the central place. As Pif circles to the second verse of

195

his March, Mother Milk-the-Cow makes the actions of milking a cow and Father Hollyberry sows wheat.

>Where is Mother Milk-the-Cow?
>Here she is, good day!

Pif bows to her, shakes her hand, and asks his question. Again he is told "Yes!" and the subsequent dialogue has the same form as with Father Hollyberry. Brother High-and-Mighty comes into the center; he chops wood during the third verse.

After a repetition of the dialogue and action, Dear Old Sister Green-Cheese joins the group. She cuts cabbages.

Fair Katie now comes into the center. During the fifth verse of the March she counts pennies from hand to hand while around her the members of her family sow wheat, milk the cow, chop wood, and cut cabbages.

Pif, hat in hand, asks Fair Katie to marry him. She says "Yes!" but only if her father, mother, brother, and sister also say "yes!" In simple action, speech, and song she tells Pif what she has to give him.

The children now stand in a circle. Pif stands alone in the center. Fair Katie, or all the class, calls rhythmically to him:

>But if I'm going to marry you,
>I must know what you can do!

The "Working Song" begins immediately as the children sing to Pif:

tai - lor? Snip - ping and snip - ping?

As they sing they make scissor movements with two fingers of one hand. Pif sings back:

Better than that! Better than that!

Hammering one fist rhythmically into the palm of the other hand, the children sing:

Are you a shoemaker
Nailing and nailing?

Pif replies as before. Following the actions of the leader, the children plow the ground before them as they ask, "Are you a farmer?""Are you a carpenter?"–they plane a piece of wood."A blacksmith?"—they swing a sledge-hammer. "A miller?"—they make windmill sails. To each question Pif sings: "Better than that!"

Everyone takes hands and circles round Pif-Paf singing:

Allegro (♩ = 72)

1 You're a be - som - bin - der! You're a be - som - bin - der!

This is the first verse of "The Besom-Binding Song." Following directions sung by the leader, the children pick the pieces of the broomcorn or twigs out of the mess and hand them to her. When it is all gathered up they return to their seats leaving Pif and the leader to make the besom.

The leader sings about each step of binding the besom while the children watch and join in the song with her. A child is asked in the song to find the stick; when he has fetched it, the broomcorn or twigs, now in a tidy bundle, are arranged around one end. Pif-Paf "holds it tight" while another child is asked to find and bring the string. With Pif-Paf holding, the leader binding, and everyone singing, the besom is bound. In the final verse, "Look! See! the besom's made!," Pif holds the besom high. The leader steps back and Pif begins to "sweep it all clean."

The pathology, age, developmental condition, and personal stamina of a handicapped child will all affect the way in which he sets about this task. One child may be able to make a well-directed beginning; another may be confused or in difficulty, and have to find his way of handling it. Pif-Paf-Poltrie's sweeping is the climax of the game; it is always a completely individual happening. From the beginning he is supported by music; the pianist accompanies him and adapts her playing of the sweeping music to the way he sweeps.

The leader stands by to give help or guidance if it is needed. From time to time the watching children sing the encouraging "Sweeping Song."

When he finishes, the children gather in a circle, Pif-Paf up-ends the besom and holds it in the center of the heap of leaves. Fair Katie takes his arm. The mood of this moment is usually serious and thoughtful. The leader asks quietly, but with rhythmic vitality:

What did Father Hollyberry say?

"Yes!" shout the children. Father Hollyberry repeats "Yes!" and steps into the center. The leader asks the question about each member of the family. The children answer with a cheer of "Yes!" each time. One by one, Mother Milk-the-Cow, Brother High-and-Mighty, and Dear Old Sister Green-Cheese step into the center to join Pif-Paf and Fair Katie. The jubilant conclusion is reached when everyone says:

They all said *yes!*
And he swept up the mess!

Pif's achievement is celebrated in a lively song. The children sing and clap to it.

They return to their seats to the final song:

Three or four of the younger, less able, or shyer children are invited to put the leaves back into the basket. The leader and pianist thank Pif-Paf-Poltrie, Fair Katie, and each child who took a leading part.

Directions

The directions are given for a team of pianist and leader. However, it is possible for a teacher to lead the game alone. In this case the directions should be adapted as appropriate. If the teacher is a musician, she can play and lead alternately; if not, she can sing the songs unaccompanied.

The game is most efficiently introduced to a group when the team, or teacher, having completely memorized it, is able to lead the children through it as through a story or play. Neither songs nor speech need to be taught beforehand but can be learned by the children as the game is repeated. Two or three sessions of this kind are usually sufficient to establish it.

Leading the Game

When you begin a Pif-Paf-Poltrie by making the mess of leaves and broomcorn or birch twigs, bear in mind the purposefulness that underlies the game—the purposefulness you want to establish as part of the children's experience. The making of the mess arouses their interest; it can have its humorous aspect, although it should never become frivolous. Manage the children's response to what you are doing to involve them in the aim of the game. Have enough leaves to make a good-sized mess, large enough to cover most of the central floor space and to be a challenge for Pif-Paf.

Before taking the besom apart, hold it up and have the children name it—this gives them pleasure; the unfamiliar word, with no associations, adds to the freshness of the game.

After the mess has been made, the child who is to be Pif-Paf-Poltrie is chosen. In the first Pif-Paf-Poltries with any group it is good to choose from the more capable boys; they may be able to speak their lines better and, when the time comes for Pif's sweeping, will probably accomplish the task with comparatively fewer difficulties. This will help you to create a clear picture of the game for the more handicapped children, or for

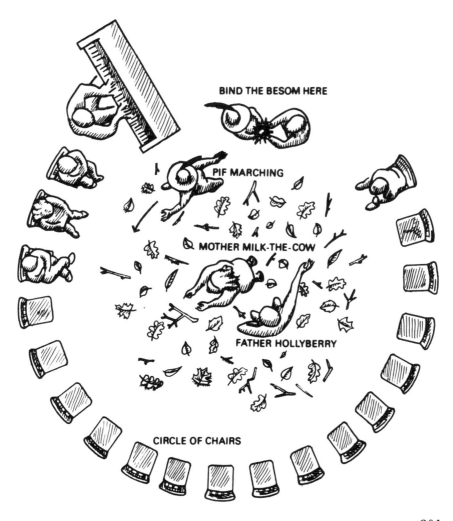

BIND THE BESOM HERE

PIF MARCHING

MOTHER MILK-THE-COW

FATHER HOLLYBERRY

CIRCLE OF CHAIRS

Fair Katie is saying her lines with purposefulness. It is therapeutic for a perceptive, nervously active child, who clowns much of the time, to focus her energies in a structured experience. Her part is important to the game and to everyone participating; it is becoming important to her. This brings some sense of responsibility which, if successfully expressed, can give her relieving feelings of seriousness and accomplishment. Although these may be fleeting impressions at first, they will affect her and deepen with repetitions of the game.

Gathering the broomcorn for Pif-Paf's besom, the children are purposeful together. This is a part of the game in which even usually inactive children like to take part. The teacher encourages an excitable, brain-injured boy who is pleased with the activity and wants to show her his part in it.

Note: See also *Therapy in Music for Handicapped Children*, pages 87–96, and for descriptions of the game with hearing impaired children *Music for the Hearing Impaired — and Other Special Groups*, pages 252–256.

those who cannot bring themselves to participate at first. These children need to be exposed to ordered experiences of the game; with each repetition of it their comprehension can grow until they are able to step into the action.

When a severely handicapped child expresses a serious wish to take the role of Pif, treat his request with the greatest respect. It may be that you would like him to be Pif and feel it would be good for him to try, yet you are not sure that he will be able to carry it through. This can be a difficult decision to make. Often a severely handicapped child can surprise even those who know him well with the strength of his goodwill and with the intensity of the efforts he makes to carry out Pif's role. Unless you are convinced that he is not yet ready to do it, you should have faith in him and be prepared to support his intention.

Fair Katie should also be chosen carefully in the beginning. A girl who can sing "Fair Katie's Song" and speak her lines with some clarity will also help to present the game clearly to the group. As you repeat it, let other girls take part until those who are more shy, withdrawn, or handicapped begin to step into the role.

As Father Hollyberry is going to be in the action throughout the first half of the game, choose a boy who will give you and Pif dependable support. He will also help to carry the action of the other characters.

The leader's opening words, which follow the "Introductory Music," start the action and set the mood. As you speak to them have in mind what the game can mean to your children, the interest it can hold for them, the adventure it will be, the pleasure it can give, the achievements it can make possible for them. Your voice will then carry warmth and seriousness, arouse feelings of anticipation, and stimulate attention and action.

The parts of Mother Milk-the-Cow, Brother High-and-Mighty, Dear Old Sister Green-Cheese, as well as that of Father Hollyberry, should be used flexibly from the beginning. All the children should feel that any one of these parts is open to them; avoid fixing a child in a part which he then plays each time you do the game. Usually, the parts of Father Hollyberry and Brother High-and-Mighty will be allotted to boys and those of Mother Milk-the-Cow and Dear Old Sister Green-Cheese to girls; but if you are short of one or the other, assign the parts to suit the group.

The game will be more alive for them if the children are chosen for the parts as the characters appear in the story. Often

204

a child watching the game will be spontaneously moved to volunteer for a part as it becomes an active reality for him, whereas he could not have done this before the game began. This first section, in which Pif-Paf meets the members of Fair Katie's family, gives opportunities to involve responding children in the various roles and to work with them so that their interest is rewarded and their confidence further strengthened.

Some children may learn to speak the characters' lines soon after the game is repeated. Others, less capable, perhaps, but with some speech facility, will require prompting and support as they attempt the speaking parts more slowly. Severely verbally handicapped children—for whom speech is almost a closed world —will need all your care and resourceful encouragement. To help each individual child as much as possible, adapt your approach to suit the abilities or difficulties he brings to the part. Kneel or sit close to him to be at his eye level, thus changing the character of your relationship to him from one who "stands over" to one who listens and helps. This will give his initiative a better chance to develop. It is also more comfortable for a child to work with you if he does not have to look up to see you.

With children who can speak well and remember the lines, prompt or correct, with as few words as possible, whenever it is needed. Should a child be slow to speak or remember, give him *time*. Don't overdirect the speech, for this will only obscure his efforts and rob him of initiative. If a child has a gross speech impediment but has remembered the part and is speaking it with pleasure and goodwill, beware of spoiling his experience by demanding that he try to enunciate more clearly. If you feel this should be done, approach him with kindness and in such a way that *your* voice shows that you recognize and appreciate his efforts, that you are going to help rather than demand. As it is almost certain that you will confront him with the handicaps of his pathology your work must have a genuinely constructive purpose.

Be conscious of the way you use your voice: it can be a most effective instrument for reaching into the personalities of handicapped children, for stimulating and encouraging them. Experiment with the inflections, the rhythms and tempos, the loudness and softness which can be brought into your voice as you work. Adjust it to the needs of each personality. Use it deliberately to evoke speech and to arouse each child's pleasure in speech. The way you speak will keep this part of the game more dynamic for the children who are watching and listening,

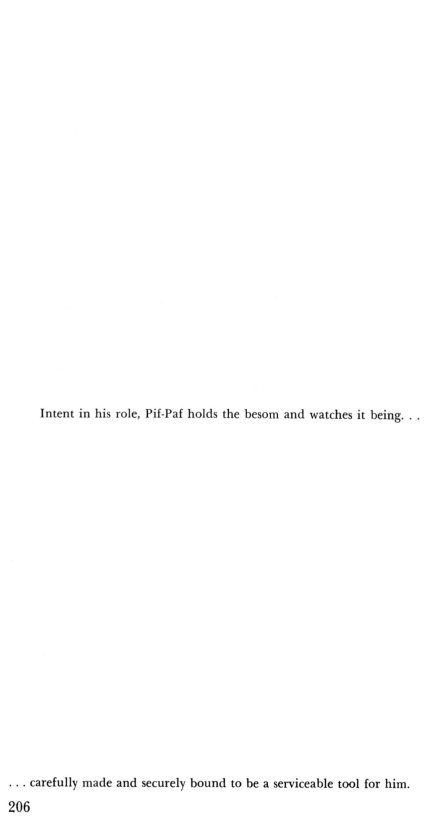

Intent in his role, Pif-Paf holds the besom and watches it being. . .

. . . carefully made and securely bound to be a serviceable tool for him.

as well as for the child with whom you are working.

You will often have to lead a more severely handicapped child through the speech part word by word. This can be delicate work and it is slow going, but when such a child puts two or three words together or speaks a whole phrase from memory, he has achieved real progress. Do not hurry him through his part because you are afraid that the rest of the class will become restless. If necessary, ask all the children to listen; it is a far better experience for everyone that you concentrate on the individual child and give him the most favorable opportunity to speak his part. Only take care that you do not overtax him, for this might destroy any confidence he is developing and his pleasure in the game.

Interest can also be brought into the speech parts by creating some interplay between the characters. This will enliven the children and also avert mechanical or rote responses. For example, have the central character, as he or she names the other members of the family, place a hand on the shoulder of each in turn, and finally a hand on Pif's shoulder to the words "Fair Katie is *yours!*" The foregoing applies to the meeting between Fair Katie and Pif-Paf.

The actions in the "Working Song" should always be made whole-heartedly. Even where the movements are small make them with vitality and precision. Into each action put the feeling of the real work it represents. This can give your movements a zestful authority that will communicate directly to the children, stimulate them, and inspire them to make their own movements with vigor and control. Take care that your movements for each action be so distinctly defined that the children's experience of each one will be vivid; then their participation will become increasingly conscious. Imagine the tool you are going to "use," take hold of it, and bring it to the working position as each verse begins. For example, in the verse "Are you a carpenter?," pick up a large wood plane and draw it back to the words "Are . . . you . . . a . . . ," ready for the strong forward drive of the plane on ". . . *car*penter"; then plane rhythmically with the rest of the verse. Similarly, for the Blacksmith, pick up a sledge-hammer and lift it up behind you to "Are . . . you . . . a . . . ," timing your movements so that the downward, beating swing of the hammer is on the accented beat of "*black*smith." Continue beating vigorously. Pif-Paf's answer, "Better than that!," to each question will often need support; the pianist can lead and encourage him.

Sing the words of the "Besom Binding Song" with rhythmic emphasis and vitality. Be conscious of each syllable; a clear enunciation of the words is more important than a good singing tone.

The essential directions for the binding of the besom are in the score. Practice binding it beforehand so that during the game you will be able to give more attention to the words of the song and to intensifying the children's interest. Bind it securely with distinct movements so that the children get the clearest picture of what is being done. Work with Pif in the gap in the circle (see the foregoing sketch) so that neither of you obstructs anyone's view more than can be avoided.

When you give Pif the untied besom to hold together—to the words "Pif-Paf-Poltrie, hold it tight!"—let him hold it alone. This can be difficult for some children, but it is intended to be a challenge. Your heart may be in your mouth as a seriously impaired or distracted, though endeavoring, Pif-Paf holds the untied broomcorn or birch twigs slackly while you are singing for the string! And he should hold it, as this is an experience that belongs to the part. If necessary, repeat "Pif-Paf-Poltrie, hold it *tight!*" dramatically, using gestures to stimulate his will and awareness.

In the sweeping up of the mess, the child who is Pif-Paf experiences both the challenge and the fulfillment of the game. As far as possible he should be left to sweep by himself. Any help he might need should be given quietly and unobtrusively. The leader's role is not to get Pif to "do it right," but to help him realize within himself the will to sweep up the mess, and then, through his own efforts, to develop the ability to do it and see it through.

Some children may need guidance to start correctly. For example, if a child is completely lost when confronted by the mess, or if his sweeping is aimless or disorganized, you must provide him with some orientation and some direction for his work. You can do this indirectly by standing in the middle of the mess and encouraging Pif to sweep toward your feet. As he moves around and sweeps, move to be opposite him so that your feet always fix the place for the heap and give him a focus for his sweeping. When a noticeable heap has begun to form or when you feel that Pif now has some idea of how to sweep, stand to one side but stay poised, observe every sweep of the broom, and be prepared to step in again if necessary.

Give your fullest attention to the way a handicapped child

"Better than that!" Pif-Paf answers the questions the children sing and the actions they make. After six questions—to which he sings the same answer—they will sing "You're a besom binder" and march around him. Adults and children alike are deep in the game—they know it will end successfully.

The boy is sweeping with care. The children have been involved in bringing this moment about and now are quietly attentive. As they watch the leaves being swept into the heap and listen to the Sweeping Music and sing the Sweeping Song, they are drawn into taking part with Pif-Paf and feeling concerned that he really does "sweep it all clean." This is part of the morality implicit in the climax of the game—the task Pif-Paf must accomplish alone, but alone only in his activity, for everyone is with him in spirit.

Jack DeFrenes, Philadelphia

Jack DeFrenes, Philadelphia

tackles Pif's sweeping. Try to feel the quality of his concentration, feel the difficulties he may be having, notice each careful act or attempt he makes. Your attentive attitude will be a great support to him and will also serve to deepen the experience of the children who are watching.

Toward the end of the sweeping there will often be the need to point out to Pif-Paf leaves that he has overlooked. Avoid using your foot to point to a leaf; pointing with the hand betokens a warmer and more caring interest. Call to him, "Pif-Paf!", to attract his attention to remaining leaves. Often the children will take it upon themselves to point out leaves in this way.

As you ask the questions "What did Father Hollyberry say?," etc., follow the indications for beginning softly and gradually getting louder. You will then succeed in changing the mood of thoughtful seriousness, with which the sweeping finishes, to the joyous tone of acclamation that leads directly into the song "Pif-Paf-Poltrie and Fair Katie." Ask these questions with controlled, rhythmic vitality. They remind everyone of Pif's progress from character to character, as they bring them back into the action of the game. Each "Yes!" should be a shout of affirmation. Let the children feel how positive all this is by the warmth of tone you put into your voice.

The leaves are gathered up after all the children, except Pif-Paf and Fair Katie, have returned to their seats to the song "And They All Lived Happily Ever After." While the song is being repeated, give the basket in which the leaves are to be replaced to a child who has not taken a leading part. Take this opportunity to invite younger, shyer, or more handicapped children to help him. Be sure that every leaf and every crumb of one is picked up and put into the basket.

The game is closed, when all the leaves are gathered up, by asking one of the leaf gatherers to take the basket to your colleague at the piano. Then thank Pif-Paf-Poltrie and congratulate him. He will appreciate your recognition of what he has done. Ask him to give his hat and besom to the pianist so that she can also thank him. Both of you thank Fair Katie. Finally go to each child who took a leading part and thank him or her sincerely.

Playing the Music

The piano should be placed so that the pianist and the children can see each other. She must observe their responses and their singing, and must be able to watch the binding of the besom, to catch and follow the leader's tempos and rhythms. It is also essential that she be able to see Pif-Paf's sweeping so that her music can accompany the tempo and character of his sweeping movements.

When Father Hollyberry has taken his place in the center of the mess and he and Pif are ready to begin the game, there should be a moment or two of silence before the "Introduction" is played. The beginning melody should be played very slowly and quietly; when the tempo doubles, in the second half of the "Introduction," the melody should still predominate. This will set the mood for the leader's opening lines.

Play "Pif-Paf-Poltrie's March" in a good, brisk walking tempo (the two notes in the first measure are in this same tempo) . Use no pedal until the very end and then only on the chord accompanying the second syllable of "Good-*Day*." Hold this chord while Pif takes off his hat and bows. Play the final chord when he puts his hat back on.

It is a great help to the children making the sowing, milking, chopping, cutting, and counting movements, as well as to those singing, if each note is equally accented. In other words, do not play the usual *one* two/*one* two, but *one two/one two*. The chords in the left hand in measures 2, 3, 4, 5 and 10, 11, 12, 13 contain good, rousing dissonances. Give these chords a firm accent and hold them throughout the measure. These dissonances are stimulating; their impelling quality keeps the music moving and supports both actions and singing; their vitality awakens vitality in children.

Bring out the melody in Fair Katie's lyric song for her to hear it as she sings. Pedal each chord. If the song is too high for her voice, play it in the key of C Major. When Pif sings his verse, hold the chord on the word "yours" as long as needed for him to place his hat on Fair Katie's head.

The "Working Song" should be accented on the first beat of the measures containing the accented syllable of each trade— Tailor, Carpenter, etc. The movements the children make to each verse grow larger as the song progresses, and call for tempo changes. The children will enjoy it if a big ritard is made in the first measure of *"Are you a/Black*smith?" and then a much slower tempo is used throughout. The staccato chord accompanying Pif's solo singing of "that," in "Better than that!," should not be so short that it ends before he has finished singing the word.

The "Besom-Binding Song" follows immediately.

Step by step, to the "Besom-Binding Song," the besom is made from the broomcorn or birch twigs the children gather, the "handy" stick and the piece of string they fetch. The pianist should know the song so well that she is able to follow the leader's singing and all the activities involved with flexibility of tempo and expression. It adds an impact to the song when she plays rhythmic patterns in the melody and harmony that match the rhythms of the words the leader introduces in the verses. If the pianist is able to use the song as a "theme" and introduce "variations" on it while keeping the outlines of the melody and harmony, she will add to everyone's pleasure. This is a happy song; it should be played with "bounce" and strict attention to phrase and staccato markings. No pedal is used. After the last verse, "Look, see, the besom's made!," there should be a moment of silence before Pif-Paf begins to sweep.

Let the phrase of each measure of the "Sweeping Music" last just as long as Pif-Paf's sweeping movement; do not play in a regular tempo but fit each measure to his sweeping in this careful way. If he stops and you feel he needs encouragement, play just a note or two of the phrase to lead him, then, when he begins to sweep, accompany him as before. However, should a child sweep very quickly you may have to simplify the music and play a single chord to each sweep. If you can adapt your playing to suit each child's sweeping, the music will support his efforts and help to maintain his concentration. Many handicapped children would be unable to carry the sweeping through without the emotional and physical encouragement the music provides. It also creates around the sweeping an individualized musical setting for the other children to experience. The sweeping music in the score is not mandatory; if the pianist is able to improvise music that has an affinity with a particular child and his sweeping, she should feel free to do so.

The "Sweeping Song" can be introduced after the heap of leaves has begun to grow or whenever the pianist, as she accompanies the child's sweeping, feels the moment is right for this song to give its lyric support to his work. It is especially stirring for him if the song is begun quite softly, a gradual crescendo made, and the repetition sung forte.

The children will need time to take a breath before singing the high E and D on the words "Pif-Paf," so make a slight pause after the word "clean."

At the end of the song, return to the "Sweeping Music." If Pif sweeps up the mess quickly, the song need be repeated only once as he finishes and then led straight into the second verse, "Gather round." But if the child is more handicapped, he may need the song sung several times as he sweeps. Repeat it as often as you feel it is needed. If the pianist is improvising freely, she can introduce song phrases into her playing using such words as:

Sweep it! Sweep it!
  Sweep it all clean
Pif-Paf-Poltrie,
  Sweep it, Pif!
Sweep it, Pif!
  Sweep it all clean!, etc.

There is no music given here. From the examples already given, the key, the harmonies and the melodic outline will serve as a guide to any teacher who wishes to have the pleasure of setting to music these words or others that seem suitable.

Pedal the chords that accompany the answering shouts of "Yes!" and hold them for two moderately slow beats. The degree of loudness with which they are played should match the volume the children use.

The song "Pif-Paf-Poltrie and Fair Katie" celebrates the achievement of the child who took the role of Pif. Play its crescendi and tempo changes exuberantly to ensure a joyful mood.

A Finnish speech therapist learns how to bind the besom, Pif-Paf helps. Birch twigs are being used—Finland's beautiful forests assure a plentiful supply. As soon as the besom is made, Pif-Paf will begin to sweep up the leaves cut out from construction paper.

Martikainen, Majalampi, Suomi-Finland

217

Play "And They All Lived Happily Ever After" affirmatively but slowly. Pedal each change of harmony. As it usually takes longer for the children to put the leaves into the basket than it does to sing this song, a coda can be improvised so that there will be music until they have finished. This can be quite simple, perhaps just the tones of the E Flat Major chord played higher in the treble to suggest the ringing of bells.

The Effects of the Game

If "Pif-Paf-Poltrie" is repeated consistently, trends of development will be observed in the children's responses. The following description of the kinds of progress that may result is based on personal experience in using the game with over 300 children and is taken also from the experiences of colleagues and graduate students. (The reports in *Therapy in Music for Handicapped Children*, pages 87–96, are particularly relevant here.)

Many severely retarded children can find in "Pif-Paf-Poltrie" an immediate social meaning and a source of stimulation that they rarely find in daily life. It appears to awaken in them a nascent desire for human purposefulness that brings them into action. Their directness of response, their conduct or concentration, their grasp of details of the game have often been astonishing. In presenting this game to these children a teacher uses an effective form of activity therapy. Its practical moral purpose, a wholesome content which they can perceive and comprehend, attracts them. The positive self-awareness these children develop in participation carries over into classroom life, as does the working relationship they form to the teacher in the game.

For many withdrawn children social experience is contaminated by associations of incapacity, distress, and/or failure. If the game is enacted objectively as activity therapy, it will be free from such damaging associations. These children will need to be led with careful support and should be treated with tenderness and tact. Quiet humor or delicate stimulation can help to further their responses; much can depend upon the way the teacher uses her voice. The withdrawn child should be able to find a growing security in the repetitions of the game and be gradually drawn into it by his own interest and pleasure. If, through his growing participation, he is led out of his state of emotional constriction, his newfound freedom will bring with it a capacity to form social relationships. This will have a broad effect upon his school life.

Some withdrawn retarded children give the impression of being remote not because they seek to shelter themselves from the pressures of life, but because of an inherent difference in their emotional lives that estranges them from other human beings. Associated with their retardation is an aloofness, a cool distancing of contact, and little use of speech. Their behavior may be calm or it may have elements of willfulness, perversity, or wildness. Such children can also respond positively to the practicality of this game, some quickly, others over a longer period of time. Often, through their participation as one of the characters or through the achievement of being Pif, they can experience the warmth of social happiness. As a result they may become more receptive in their independence, and some will form friendships.

Restless or distracted children find the structure of the game as a whole, or any part they may be asked to take in it, a disturbing challenge to their usual mode of behavior. This can be an extremely good thing—the beginning of therapy—provided that the teacher, as she works to lead such a child into participation, is sympathetic to his pathology and does not overtax whatever capacity for self-control he has. These children differ in the amount of challenge they need or can endure. In working with them there may be times when the teacher has to be firm, to emphasize the seriousness of the work that she and the other children are doing. But she will find that asking for good behavior for the sake of the ongoing game has a different effect from demanding it for the usual reasons. Therapy for these children lies in the repetitions of the game; in its variety of moods and activities are contrasts of experience that engage them; they find security in its definite structure and in the constancy of its purpose, which, in time, they can relate to themselves. Participation becomes by degrees a source of shared experience and pleasure unmarred by the effects of old behavioral impulses. When a distracted child reaches the point of being Pif and is able—even with difficulty—to carry the role through, some improved behavioral responses are usually established.

The combination of retardation and pronounced emotional disturbance is an extremely tragic affliction for a young human being to bear. Each retarded child with a serious emotional problem is caught in a complex of difficulties. These are demanding for a teacher to cope with for his behavior is often bizarre, anti-social, and/or destructive. But such a child may suffer from a pathetic need for an enduring human regard and warmth. The teacher can offer these personal expressions of her goodwill to him in the way she leads him into the structure of the game. Then her compassion is not in danger of being lost in subjectivity; it becomes, instead, part of the child's experience of the course and content of the game. This objectively directed warmth is usually far more acceptable to him. It can, for example, be expressed in the care with which she helps him sustain his participation in such a role as Brother High-and-Mighty. All the short, clearly defined roles of the "family" can be helpful to these children, for they are experiences of social activities for which a pattern of conduct is laid down. As emotionally disturbed children are so often responsive to music, it is supportive to them that in this section of the game music frames and enlivens each character's part.

When an emotionally disturbed child gets to the point of taking on the role of Pif-Paf, the mood of the whole game is likely to be electric. The teacher will feel the drama he brings into the "Pif situation," for his urge to do it will often be in conflict with his emotional impairment; she may have to be dramatic herself in her leading. Pif-Paf-Poltrie's sweeping is very critical for such a child. Emotional instability and confusion fight against the purposefulness and orderliness the sweeping requires. If, despite all help, the child balks at the sweeping, goes to pieces, or gives up, he should be asked to choose someone else to be Pif for him. He should give the besom and the hat to the new Pif and then sit to watch him sweep. This changeover should be made as positively as possible. The child should feel the teacher's appreciation for the attempt he has made, her objective acceptance of his failure, and her understanding of his difficulties. He can be given another opportunity to be Pif later, when it is felt that he is better able to succeed.

Should such a child carry the part all the way through, this will be a considerable triumph for him. As a result of this achievement the teacher may attain a deeper and more reliable personal relationship with him. He may be more relaxed in social relationships, perhaps more at ease with regard to partici- pation in classroom objectives.

Chapter Six

The Rewards Live

David

David was an inactive, self-effacing mongoloid, 7 years old, who had started school in September. In November, when the project began, his teacher told us she thought David must be deaf. He had done nothing but sit with his legs under him for two months. He did not respond when his name was called or show any interest in classroom activities. When we gave him the drum to beat to improvised music, his beating was soft, tremulous, unrhythmic, and he could not beat in regular time to the music.

During the first "Pif-Paf-Poltrie" with David's class, I called his name softly as he passed the piano when the children were circling the principal characters. He turned his head toward me —he was obviously not deaf. We noticed that he was paying some attention to the action; once or twice he showed signs of quiet pleasure in it.

When we were repeating "Pif" for the fourth time, three weeks later, David raised his hand—timidly, shoulder high—to take the part of Brother High-and-Mighty. This was a big step for such a silent, inactive boy. The following week he volunteered, in the same timorous way, to be Pif.

We had watched David's interest deepen, and his participation become more active in each repetition of the game. We had waited for his initiative to take him this far. From the beginning of the game he was carefully conscious of what he was doing; he knew the music and the actions, and it was obvious he wanted to do Pif as well as he could. In his meetings with the other characters he was the personification of gentleness. When he swept he expressed care and thoroughness. Mongoloid children seem to have a special relationship to "Pif-Paf-Poltrie"; their faith and belief in it, their objective commitment to it, are always impressive to see.

David made musical progress during the work with "The Three Bears." His coordination and sense of tempo improved so much that he became a dependable Father Bear. He kept his eyes on the conductor, he knew his cues, knew the story. His slow bowing when the bears were rubbing their eyes was masterful. Being able to play rhythmically in tempo opened a world of musical experience for him.

He became responsive to classroom activities, showing some assertiveness and a quiet sense of humor. At home he was more communicative; he expressed his pleasure in the musical activities and was proud of the parts he played.

Later, a national tragedy occurred a few days before we were due at the school, and when we arrived the children were all disturbed. They surrounded us to tell us what had happened. During the assembly that morning I improvised a calm, serious, memorial hymn. The words were very simple: "God bless you. God bless you. God be with you. God be with you. Amen." Every week thereafter David came to me quietly and said one word, "God." I would take his hand and with his index finger play the melody of the hymn. It is still David's special song.

P.N.

Edward

The cymbal part in "A Message for the King" is very demanding; there is hardly a repetition of similar rhythmic structure a child can lean on. Instead there are many variations of pattern that call for a different use of the instrument each time. Edward was an orphan who had lived in a succession of foster homes. He was a good-willed boy, but filled with indecision. Directed to do something, he would come back to be told again, just to make sure; and a few seconds later he would return again, this time with a suggestion that he do a different thing or change, in some way, the original request.

We decided to see what he would do with the cymbal part. In the first rehearsals he had to struggle against these old habits; many times he would raise his arm and on cue begin the down-

224

ward stroke to crash the cymbal accurately on the beat—he had a good sense of rhythm—only to check himself at the last split second and arrest the stroke. This showed his lack of self-confidence, the indecision that was his normal mode of life. It had led to an unfulfillment which engendered inattention and little habits of perversity; many times during the rehearsals, when it was his turn to play, he would be sitting, quite unprepared, looking out the window or trying to catch another child's attention.

But he was musical, and as we worked and repeated sections, insisting on precision, he gradually developed a kind of loyalty to the work and became dependable. He was given a second instrument, a small gong which was to be played on the unaccented beats of a fairly complex rhythmic pattern. He had to change fairly quickly from the cymbal to the gong. We told him that when the word "Queen" was spoken in the narrative he was to pick up the gong and be ready to play; he soon learned to do this on his own initiative. Almost always when I turned to Edward to lead his gong playing, I found him poised and ready, all his attention fixed on me. Edward showed more purposefulness in the classroom and a very touching devotion to his musical activities. We felt that he knew he needed them. C.R.

Patti

Patti was a lightly built, sweet, passive, 8-year-old. She had the low-pitched, indistinct singing voice typical of mongoloid children and was able to sing only one or two tones near Middle C in pitch. She was particularly fond of instrumental activities and had enjoyed playing a bell part in the orchestra of "The Children's Christmas Play." After a year of working with a variety of musical instruments, she was given the part of Baby Bear in "The Three Bears." Patti made this her part; to hold that quarter-sized violin, to take her—Baby Bear's—place in the group, to work on her playing within the musical structure of the whole, became a way through which she could bring herself into focus. It was a way of concentrating, of living in the functioning of her memory, and of enjoying herself and her friends in the sheer pleasure of the activity.

225

She held the violin as if she and it were a single musical being—a professional musician, seeing her at work in a film of "The Three Bears," remarked that her playing position was almost perfect.

Patti became ever more lively and alert. She developed a sturdy independence in her school life. Her teacher was thrilled with her growth and with the bounce and humor that had appeared in her social life.

Two years later in an assembly, we heard a new singing voice—lovely, warm, true. It was Patti! She was singing in the group with unselfconscious pleasure. But when we asked her to sing a solo, her new voice was not there. It was too soon to ask her to use it consciously and deliberately.

What had developed and freed Patti's singing? Was it the violin tone she had produced so many times—a clear, high D″ so close to her, penetrating her body and mind? All the music in which she had played must have sounded to her in relationship to that tone. Perhaps it had created a *tonal center* for her musical experience; she must have held memories of it, both conscious and unconscious. This tone was completely and essentially associated with the personality growth resulting from her work in "The Three Bears." She had developed a sense of tonal relationship and this, with her firmly grounded confidence in musical activities, plus her pleasure in the songs she knew so well, made it possible for her really to sing.

So many trainable children make their important responses from some deep and individual part of the psyche. These emerge in the warmth of a child's response but are unestablished to begin with. They are forward leaps of personality development and can be all too easily checked if too much is made of them, too much direct attention paid to them. It is better to work indirectly, when improvements first appear, and to let the child's new ability become his conscious possession through his own use of it, his pleasure in it. Once it is established in this way, we can take the child further through activities that will express our acknowledgment of his newfound ability and our delight in it, without running the risk of linking it to old patterns of response and behavior stemming from the child's pathology.

P.N.

226

Allen

Allen was a perceptive mongoloid who was cripplingly sensitive to his disabilities. He had a severe speech impairment and rarely spoke; when he did, it was only a single word. But we understood each other and worked well together. When "The Children's Christmas Play" was first developed he was given a horn part in the orchestra. He liked to blow it; he was attentive and co-operative at rehearsals.

At the first dress rehearsal, when the cast walked in procession into the auditorium and up to the stage, the orchestra saw the players in their costumes for the first time. Allen turned pale. He left his place on the orchestra platform, shuffled to where his teacher was sitting, and said his first sentence: "I can't." He was overwhelmed by the experience, and not yet having found any confidence in himself and really despairing, he had given up. The positive aspect of this, for his teacher and for us, was that *he had been able to express his feelings.* We let him stay where he was, and with encouragement he played his horn part from there. Later, his teacher wrote out his full name in large letters on a strip of paper. This was put on his chair in the orchestra. At the next rehearsal he was back in place and played his part well. His mother reported that, during the time of the rehearsals and performance, he was speaking more at home.

Some months later he volunteered, with a quiet happiness, to be Pif. The defeat and nervousness that lay behind the "I can't" were disappearing. He was becoming self-confident, holding his head high and moving differently. He was more observant and was acting sociably, with kindness. He began to eat a variety of food—his main diet for years had been bread spread with butter and mustard. His speech was still extremely limited but he was now facing the problem of verbal communication with a responsive goodwill. He sustained this objectivity in the dialogues in "Pif-Paf-Poltrie." His sweeping was perfect. The game continued to be important to him in all the years we worked at the school.

The following year Allen was one of the Shepherds in "The Christmas Play." Two years later, in the middle of a rehearsal, after all the cast had been chosen (he was to be a King) he went onto the stage and took the position and posture of the Angel; in this way he let us know he wanted to play this part. It was one of the leading roles and included the singing of a carol to awaken the Shepherds. We felt his wish to be so important that we rearranged several children's parts to give him the opportunity. Allen's courageous performance was memorable. At times during the action other players had to guide him quietly through his part, but this did not defeat him—he carried it through with reverence and deep seriousness.

Allen continued to develop as he grew older and taller. He showed an understanding perception of a situation and—although he certainly could not describe this verbally, or think in abstract terms about it—he could respond with an action that was just right, perfectly suited to the occasion.   P.N.

Eddie

Eddie was the most cautious, self-protective, easily frightened boy in the school. But the day came when he asked to be Pif. Willing but grave, he sought my hand at the "Introduction" of the game and continued to hold it on his first march around. He raised his hat to Father Hollyberry with a serious, straight face. When the second verse of the "March" began, he reached out again for my hand. But this time I indicated with a gesture that he should march alone. To everyone's astonishment he did. When he raised his hat to Mother Milk-the-Cow his face broke into a smile. With each progressive meeting the smile grew broader, his face more relaxed and happy.

He held the besom well for the binding and then swept deliberately and carefully for almost ten minutes. Eddie's establishment of himself in the role against the background of his usual fear-ridden, unsure behavior and his independent display of initiative and courage were totally unexpected and could not have been predicted. His teacher said: "Well, he's graduated!" None of us had ever seen him so active; the usual fear-begotten toilet accidents that had accompanied previous activities did not occur.   C.R.

Diane

Diane was in a class of educable girls. She was 14, very tall, rather aloof, shy, and self-conscious, probably because of her height. When we began the project, Diane refused to participate in any instrumental activity. She would not sing with us. One day we introduced the resonator bells. She couldn't resist them. She obviously enjoyed playing them and became really involved in the intimate tonal experiences the bells gave her.

When we came to work on the setting of the "Twenty-Third Psalm," Diane was given the resonator bell part. Although we had but one rehearsal weekly, she soon knew which bells to get out of the case, and in what order to arrange them on the table. She learned to follow the notes from the score we made especially for her. She was very proud of her score and took it home each week. She seldom made a mistake and then only from nervousness.

When the Psalm was well learned, the girls performed it several times in public. It gave everyone great pleasure and was warmly applauded. Diane's new self-image and self-confidence stimulated both academic and social improvement. Her teacher requested a psychological evaluation. She did well on these tests and was transferred into a regular class.   P.N.

Denise

Sometimes a trainable child will sit and watch the other children in musical activities for many weeks and not take part. Denise was a quiet, retiring child who would occasionally corner and frighten younger or more helpless children. She would watch the work with some interest, at times rocking gently, but whenever offered a part she would smile weakly and refuse. One day, when the girl who was playing Three Drums in "The Three Bears" was absent, we asked Denise to do it. As usual, she refused. We insisted, the children coaxed her, and finally she stood, stick in hand, behind the drums. He face showed how tense she was and we could feel, behind her unassertive nature, a hidden, debilitating lack of confidence. I was prepared to work hard to teach her the part. But there was no need; her retiring behavior was also hiding a high degree of perceptivity and musical intelligence, which she had not the courage to put to use. Each time the music called for her part she played it perfectly. Her rhythmic precision was remarkable. She surprised and impressed us all. In the weeks following we discovered that Denise knew every part in the work; of greater importance was the fact that *she* made the same discovery, she experienced the range of her own abilities.

Later Denise took the role of Mary in "The Children's Christmas Play." This had a beneficial effect on her marked speech impairment, for through the work on her lines she gained a more objective feeling about using her voice. Two of her close friends had been Mary in previous performances; that she was now playing this part established her in the social life of the school. After the performance Denise was no longer personally inhibited. She became talkative, expressed her pleasure in the musical activities, and was a loyal, perceptive colleague in all the demonstration work with teachers we did the following year.

C.R.

Phil

Phil was frightened of everything, thin, nervous, and sheltered by an overprotective mother; he was given the part of the leading Shepherd in the first performance of "The Children's Christmas Play." At rehearsals he said his line with understanding and good timing, but usually so softly he could be heard only by those nearby. We worked to give him the courage to speak with more force. At the performance he came down the aisle, yawning and stretching, with the other sleepy Shepherds, said his line, "There's a good place, let's sleep there," in a loud voice, and burst into tears. While the play went on I knelt down with him and drew his attention to the animals in the barn and to the arrival of Mary and Joseph. The action and the music drew him back into the play and he was able to continue.

This experience was the beginning of freedom for Phil; he became more outgoing, more responsive and active in class, lost his fearfulness, and developed so far that he became one of our most gifted and dependable musicians. He was later reevaluated and moved into the educable classes. C.R.

230

Cathy

Cathy was very quick and bright for a trainable child. She had good speech, and she was musical. Her extreme nervousness, plus a desire to show that she understood and could do what was required, caused her to begin everything too soon. She would start to sing as soon as the name of the next song was announced, before the pianist could begin to play. She would begin to speak her lines, for example, in "Pif-Paf-Poltrie," before the other child had finished his. When standing in the game or in the orchestra with a part to speak or play, Cathy had to touch her right leg below the knee with her right hand, constantly. This was a kind of nervous compulsion.

Cathy learned to play the final glissando of the Goldilock's Shadow part in "The Three Bears" in a special way. Slowly, plucking each string of the toy harp one after the other, she had to use real physical and emotional control to make the required musical effect. Heretofore she had been impelled to make very rapid, meaningless strummings all through the song. Now each glissando became more meaningful, and the last a special challenge and pleasure for her. This was a great gain.

To regulate her speech in "The Children's Christmas Play," musical phrases were specially composed to precede each line she was to speak, to give her tempo, inflection, and dynamics. She learned to wait and take her cue from the music. This and a succession of structured instrumental activities that she could confidently master dispelled her nervousness. Her nervous habits ceased.   P.N.

Cynthia

Cynthia had been coming to school for less than four months. Her teacher said that she had never spoken in school, although her mother said the child spoke at home. There seemed some doubt about this in the teacher's mind; we saw that Cynthia's failure to speak was a source of conflict in the classroom. In the few weeks we worked in that school we did a number of "Pifs," some work with resonator bells and simple instruments. Early one morning we had just placed the basket, and Pif's hat and his besom, on the floor outside the door of our storeroom. Cynthia rounded the corner on her way to the toilet. She looked down, then said—partly to herself, partly to us—"that belongs to Pif-Paf-Poltrie."

The musical activities for Cynthia were experiences which invited and didn't threaten, which stimulated without putting her on the spot. P.N.

Jimmy

One day, in assembly, a very short, stolid mongoloid boy raised his hand to sing a solo verse to the song "What Shall We Do with the Dog? He barks all day/And he barks all night!" Any child who wanted to sing this was free to choose the animal he would sing about. Jimmy sang thoughtfully: "What Shall We Do with My Girl Friend?" (she was an older, tall, glamorous girl) ; and then: "She walks all day/And she walks all night."

That Jimmy had the originality to use the song in this way was a big surprise—no one had ever done this before; that he could integrate his concept of this girl's relaxed, springy walk with the form of the song showed his imagination and intelligence. Songs can often provide opportunities for such expressions of a child's feeling and thinking. C.R.

Mike

Mike was cerebral palsied, spent all his day in a wheelchair, and found it impossible to speak except at home to his mother, and in speech therapy. We gave him the role of The Sick Man in "The Story of Artaban."

In this part he had only to groan. The sounds he made at the beginning were so faint they could hardly be heard. Finally at one rehearsal he groaned more loudly. The children were thrilled. "I heard him! I heard him!" they said excitedly. At the performance Mike's groans were loud enough to be heard at the back of the hall!

Having performed successfully and been appreciated by the others, Mike felt a kinship with them and a certain pride in belonging to this group. The play had impressed the audience, and the players were aware of this. Mike must have become less overwhelmed by his incapacities, for when we began to work freely in the classroom with the story of "Dummling and the Golden Goose," he began to speak. We treated this story as a comedy to relax the children after their serious work. In this easy, playful atmosphere, Mike, as the Little Old Grey Man, spoke surprisingly freely and enjoyed exchanging his lines with the other characters.

Later, when we reassembled the cast of "Artaban" in order to make a recording of it, he had made such progress that we could give him, as The Sick Man, an important line to say: "Look for Him in Bethlehem." He did this well. Speech had always been difficult for Mike, and his speech therapy was hard work; his mother told us that he was experiencing for the first time, in his roles in the plays, the pleasure of using speech.   C.R.

Larry

Larry could not bear to make a mistake; he was vastly oversensitive to failure. When he failed at anything he would become completely demoralized, hide his face in his hands, and sulk. We had a difficult time with him, for his nervousness robbed him of what capacities he had and he was unable to experience objectively what he was being asked to do. This was a serious impairment to his general progress because it kept his attention focused uneasily upon himself.

Larry began to enjoy the music and was attracted by the instruments. He would take an instrumental part with something like enthusiasm, but his pleasure in holding the instrument came more from his turn in the limelight than from any grasp of what he was going to do with it. He was still playing at "acting success" in a very immature way. When it was his turn to play, the inevitable mistakes brought back the insecurity and the tears.

Although we understood Larry's predicament to some extent and gave him all the encouragement we could, we did not show sympathy for his failures. Part of Larry actually enjoyed the misery these brought on—this was himself as he had always known himself, this was the source of the comfort and consoling tenderness he received at home.

But Larry's musical intelligence began to awaken to the musical compositions on which his class was working. At the same time he began to feel the objective quality of the working spirit of the whole music project and was affected by observing the participation of many of his classmates. There came a day when he tried an important and dramatic instrumental part; he was to give a large bell a single clang on the first beat of every measure in the "King's Music" from "The Children's Christmas Play." He began to play but soon made a mistake. For the first time, with a nervous urgency in his voice he said, "All right, all right, I try again!" He did try, harder than before, and with some helpful guidance played his part correctly through the long piece of music. He had realized that the music he liked depended on the efforts he made, and his wish to make the music with the pianist and with his schoolmates in the orchestra overcame his old, habitual reaction to challenge. This was an important act in Larry's development, the beginning of a more mature attitude toward his own life, and the appearance of self-reliance and courage in his personality.

Never again did mistakes completely defeat him and he would always "try again." Even so, his sensitivity to failure was so deeply rooted that it was 18 months before his experiences and achievements in group musical work freed him entirely from this fear.

It is doubtful that anyone seeing him playing the Owl's part in the film "Group Musical Activities," and beating the drum in "A Message for the King," in the same film, would realize his former difficulties. Larry is now an adolescent, but he lacks that mood of uncertainty and resignation that burdens so many handicapped adolescents. His attitude is positive and happy.

P.N.

Gail

Gail was 7 years old, a plump hemiplegic child. Her rather small eyes expressed a good bit of shrewdness and intelligence. She was very stubborn. With shrewdness and stubbornness she had succeeded in subduing her parents.

The time came for her to enter school. Her reaction was to scream at the top of her lungs during the entire bus trip. She screamed in protest all day long in the classroom. It was absolutely impossible to quiet her; the bus driver, the bus matron, the children on the bus and in her classroom, and—last but far from least—the patient, suffering teacher were being driven out of their minds by Gail's piercing yells. After several days of this ordeal her parents were asked to keep her at home.

We heard this story some months later when we began the fourth year of music therapy with the children and teachers of this school. Gail's desperate mother had asked the principal to give her daughter another chance. The principal had stipulated that she bring the child herself and remain in school to help acclimate her or to take her home if necessary. Gail's return coincided with ours.

We heard her begin to scream the moment she arrived in the classroom. We heard her on our way to the auditorium, where we were to have an assembly. She was to stay in another room with her mother until this was over. I thought music could be a way of getting her settled into school life. Feeling it was now or never, I fetched and brought her yelling loudly into the auditorium. We began and went on with the assembly. Some children were annoyed, others were oppressed by Gail's yells, but as we paid her no attention, they followed our lead. Her piercing screams gradually subsided to a more normal crying. Then she stopped entirely and stared at the ceiling. We continued our work on the children's singing. Suddenly Gail began to sing. She sang the words haphazardly but on pitch. At the end of the assembly she went to the piano and played single tones forcefully with a stiff, straight finger—"I'm helping you," she said.

I had to go upstairs to the music room to prepare the instruments for a class and took Gail with me. She began to yell again and ask for her mother. As I worked I echoed her and began to sing, somewhat derisively, "She wants her Mommy, she wants her Mommy, all the time." Gail stopped crying immediately and listened, again staring at the ceiling. I improvised other verses and when I repeated "She wants her Mommy," she gave a short chuckle. I sang part of the phrase and stopped—Gail completed it. We were silent for a while; every time she began to ask for her mother I sang again and she stopped to listen.

The class came in and we worked with the instruments. Gail was abstracted but was no behavior problem—she seemed to be compelled to listen to any musical sound. Later we discovered that she had taken in something of the children's work although she had not seemed to be paying much attention to it at the time.

Gail did not cry the rest of that day. She did not scream or yell in school again. She enjoyed assemblies and music activities. It took her a few weeks to accept coming to school on the bus.

C.R.

Conclusion

When you begin a music therapy program, be aware from the first session onward that you are working *in time* and *with time*. Plan to hold regular music therapy sessions throughout the months to come and anticipate them as "spaces" to be filled with the richness of work and with development in the children. Carry the sessions through consistently, repeating and developing the musical activities and working resourcefully with the children's responsiveness. You will then be initiating and maintaining *processes of therapeutic growth*. Session by session the children's experiences will intensify and their participation become animated and more extensive. Abilities you had not foreseen will begin to emerge; capacities for understanding and for concentrated work will appear. All these developments will be caught up in the content of the work itself and carry it further.

Music therapy should never be thought of as a static or routine activity, but as an up-building, evolving process. This perspective will give flexibility to your approach. As you work with the children, be aware that for almost all of them you are creating the foundations for developments beyond their initial responses. You must give yourself entirely to the work of the moment—whatever special demands it may make—if these future developments are to be secured, yet never lose sight of the mounting and growing nature of the work. Although you will often have to challenge children to intensify their activity, equally often you will need to give them time: time for their experiences to stabilize and deepen, time for their memories to work on their experiences and transform them into understanding and ability.

If you work with music therapy in this spirit, time will be on your side.

As the sessions are repeated and the activities build up, children who did not take part because they were emotionally impaired or less capable begin to be drawn into them. There will be occasions when you will be joyfully amazed by what these children, who have learned by watching and listening, will do. The structure of the music will have made sense to them and their musical intelligence will have begun to grasp a particular musical part. It can happen that a severely handicapped child will want to play, for example, two beats on a drum in answer to two chords on the piano. The severity of his handicap may hinder his execution, but as you watch him trying you will perceive that in some way, at some level, his consciousness has grasped the form of the part, and he is struggling against gross inner impairments to express it.

Avoid taking the attitude "It will be a long time before this child learns his part." Work with him with respect for his great efforts. He is endeavoring to make connections between his mind and body which, because of disuse, have never been developed. When he achieves success he will have done far more than "learn his part." His ego drive will have broken through the tangle of impairment and made some of his capacities his own; he will have expressed himself, his will, and his intelligence. He will have taken a step in *self-realization*. The circumstances under which this beachhead of personality was established—the music and the musical working situation—will be very special to him.

The work at any stage is full of living rewards but especially so when a complete musical composition begins to grow and become a reality through the combined and various developments of the children involved. It is the music, the composition, that arouses their efforts, that gives them a field of experience, and affords the scope for their widening activities and growth. It is the mutual dedication to, and enjoyment of, the piece of music itself which you share with the children, that unites your efforts, that makes a human bond of your daily work and the developments the children achieve.

All too often children become accustomed to the everyday, the commonplace, the second-rate in the music they hear. Many children believe this is what they want because this is all they know.

Music is a language, and for children it can be a stimulating language, a consoling language. It can encourage, hearten, delight, and speak to the inmost part of the child. Music can ask stimulating questions and give satisfying answers. It can activate and then support the activity it has evoked. The right music, perceptively used, can lift the handicapped child out of the confines of his pathology and place him on a plane of experience and response where he is considerably free of intellectual or emotional dysfunction. (The idea that the brain-injured or mentally deficient have a "primitive" consciousness and that the music used with them should be on a primitive level negates the whole potential of music therapy.)

This language of music, when used as therapy, must be "spoken" with consciousness, care, and discrimination. Just as ordinary speech—incorrectly or carelessly used—will fail in communication, so will the language of music fail to establish communication and fail to activate when it is meager in quality and ineffectively performed.

Consider the paucity of the emotional lives of these children: some of them are always sad, heavy, melancholy; others seem happy but in a meaningless way; still others are distractible and wild. Whether sad, blurred, bizarre, or dreamy, the child's emotional life is an essential attribute of his present self. With the best of intentions you cannot give him your feelings about life, or about him, nor can you easily make him feel the things you feel. But if you can *share* experiences—and the arts are shared experiences, are languages by which feelings are communicated —then you and he can feel the same thing, can be in emotional rapport. In the new feelings engendered by his new experiences he will find a new freedom. He may not experience the freedom itself, but he does express his free activity, his own will in the musical working situation. This experience stays, becomes a new component of his emotional life, and grows!

When music therapy activities include works that are so big and above the ordinary that they transform the everyday teacher-child relationship, a child becomes engrossed in his part in the work because you are engrossed in it; you become partners, two human beings who are going to perform a work together. The child has an objective relationship to you which is part of the freedom in activity he experiences.

Pathology isolates. Each child becomes, to a greater or lesser extent, isolated in his condition, in his lack of development; he identifies himself with his difficulties. Group music therapy, through its power to envelop all the children in a single experience, to unite their efforts in its activities and results, breaks down the isolation and with it many of the pathological impediments to development.

Children's emotional vitality needs special forms of activity; these, too, can be found in the arts, most particularly in music and drama. Just as the discharge of physical energy into the right activities, under the guidance of a qualified teacher, builds healthy bodies, skills, well-being, and purposefulness, so can the stimulation, discharge, and channeling of emotional energies build strong, well-balanced personalities. Artistic activities do this work from *within* the child. His individuality is directly affected by and involved in musical or dramatic activity; the content and tone of his feelings change as his emotional energy finds creative, intercommunicative channels of expression.

In music therapy we are vitally concerned with reducing the burden of the child's pathology. We aim to release him from his confinement not merely for an hour or two each week in the music room, but to try, through the results of our work, to lessen his handicap effectively and permanently. If we can change his responsiveness, his awareness of himself, his attitude to others, we can set him on a new course of development that may result in an entirely different, more positive life for him.

These aims may appear to be overambitious, but all therapy must have such positive goals. Certainly any significant therapeutic developments we are able to initiate in a seriously impaired child during his early years in school can have both long-term and far-reaching results. We in special education share these responsibilties for we are working for the whole future of human beings and for the human relationships they will form throughout their lives.

Appendix 1

Group Instrumental Activities for Physically Disabled Children

Practical Requirements

In every group of physically disabled children, different kinds and degrees of incapacity for using musical instruments will be present. Some children will be able to handle one instrument or even a variety of instruments well, while for others, more heavily handicapped, special adaptations or developments of instruments may have to be made. For each child an instrument should be available that will enable him to make a successful entrance into group music making. A wide selection of instruments, such as described in the chapter on instrumental group activities, gives the therapist a choice of means with which to meet particular physiological conditions with creative resourcefulness. To this selection a number of special considerations apply and some helpful additions can be made:

Two or three drums with rounded edges (such as the conga type), sounding contrasting pitches, will be necessary. These are for children who are unable initially to hold or control drumsticks and who must therefore use their hands, as best they can, for beating. The rounded edges of such drums are kinder to the hands when spasticity, athetosis, or lack of coordination cause disordered movements.

Often the musical effect of a drum beat is marred by a child's inability to lift his hand or beater off the drumhead after hitting it. A tambourine is usually more percussively effective in such instances.

A variety of beaters and drumsticks of different lengths, thicknesses, weights, and balances will facilitate choosing the one most satisfactory for a child. It may be necessary in some cases to wrap the handle of a beater with foam rubber or cloth to give a better grip.

241

For the playing of a cymbal, resonator bell, gong, or drum, a useful aid may be devised by the adaptation of a single piano action—one key, complete with its mechanism and hammer, mounted on a baseboard—precisely the kind of model used in piano showrooms to demonstrate a piano's action. The instrument to be played should be attached to the action's frame by clamps or specially arranged brackets, so that the surface to be struck is held where the piano string would normally lie in relation to the hammer. Both the mechanisms of upright and grand pianos may be used for this purpose; the grand piano action is more suitable for striking a suspended cymbal. In both types, the damping mechanism should be removed. This special instrument makes it possible for young or severely disabled children to produce completely satisfactory musical sounds or beats simply by making some kind of striking contact with the key or by putting pressure on it in some way. Children who have never been able to experience successful musical participation may first realize this through such a means. Unhindered by the difficulties attendant in using the finer coordination required to play a cymbal or resonator bell with a beater, they can often achieve a surprisingly accurate and satisfying placement of tone or beat. Once this initial experience has been established, the meaningfulness of instrumental activity can light up for a child, and he may well go on to show a perceptive motivation and purposefulness in attempting to use instruments in the direct, conventional way.

The achievement of initial successful involvement for children who are unable to use their arms adequately may make it necessary to develop, experimentally, other mechanical aids utilizing movements of the head, trunk, or foot. An excellent sourcebook in this area is: *Clinically Adapted Instruments for the Multiply Handicapped*, listed in *Appendix 4*.

Blowing instruments will be found especially important, since they can deepen breathing, where this is shallow, and since many children will possess more facility at first for using a blowing instrument than a percussive one. The instrument can be held for a child when necessary. Reed horns are simple, practical, and effective for this work. When a child is unable to close his mouth around the mouthpiece of a horn, a Melodica may be found more suitable, the required key (s) being held down for the child if he cannot do it himself. Should a child be able to finger a Melodica but not in the usual position, the extension, "stepped" mouthpiece, which lowers the instrument from the

242

Kiniken for Cerebral Parese—

She plays a drum and cymbal alternately. The piano-action cymbal beater assures a successful, stimulating cymbal crash; as she hits the key, spasticity prevents her from lifting her arm, but the operation of the piano mechanism causes the hammer to drop back after striking the cymbal, leaving its tone unimpaired. At this stage, the therapist's music supports her as she concentrates on the contrast of sounds she creates. Her simple, large movements become more harmoniously directed and increasingly regular in rhythm.

og Børneneurlogi, Copenhagen

mouth, or the extension tube designed to enable the instrument to be played on a table, may make its use practicable. With the extension tube, the Melodica can be placed in any position suitable for the child's arm-hand facility.

For a severely incapacitated child, an instrument can be created by hanging one bell or several bells of different pitches from a bar or other support held or placed where he can reach them in some way with his arm, elbow, shoulder, head, nose, etc. He need but touch, knock, or push the bells to ring them. The bells should possess good musical tonal qualities and produce a volume of sound which will be significant for the child. Cow, goat, and sheep bells cast in brass or bronze are particularly effective, being warm and sonorous in the bass and vibrantly clear in the treble.

Goals and the Working Approach

All the general therapeutic goals of instrumental group activities described in Chapters 2 and 3 apply directly to work with physically disabled children, as do all the musical and practical principles set forth. The special circumstances arising from work with physical disabilities, in which music making must become a reality despite individual handicaps in the group, make creative empiricism a necessity. The therapist's initial aims are to achieve a genuinely musical result involving the coactive response of the group through the simplest possible means. This *musicality of intention* in the practical work is of fundamental importance, for it is in the quality of a child's pleasure in musical activities— in his interest, his active commitment and confidence—that all developmental processes in music therapy originate, both psychotherapeutically and physiotherapeutically.

Psychotherapeutic processes involving self-realization, personal enrichment, and social growth for the physically disabled occur, as discussed throughout this book, in response to the form and character of the activities. They also result immediately from any enlargement of physical capacity. Physiotherapeutic developments are initiated when the vitalness and warmth of active musical engagement carry new stimulations for expression, participation, or discovery that quicken and change a child's inner attitude toward the use of his body. For a young child, this may be an awakening to the very possibility of effective, satisfying action; as he pursues this, a measure of control and organization of movement may evolve spontaneously out of his involvement in the rhythmic organization of a particular piece of music. In a

244

Geelsgaard Kostskole, Copenhagen

Muscular dystrophy robs him of the strength to raise his arms and hands so that he is unable to play a Melodica held to his mouth. He can use it with the aid of the tube attachment, playing melodies with his thumbs and index fingers.

245

somewhat older child, a drive to accomplish the movements required to play an instrument—to bow a cello or violin, for example—can first be spurred and then supported by his concentration on the character of the musical experience his playing creates in the context of an arrangement (and also by the beauty and character of the instrument). An adolescent can find personal fulfillment in instrumental activities that create musical experiences appropriate for his age. As he plays, the musical-structural-emotional goals of his efforts take on a personal significance which displaces any insecurity or resignation, apathy, or self-protectiveness he may feel and incites a more persistent will to achieve—and possibly, in achieving, to realize some degree of capacity hitherto undeveloped.

Deeply involved in all instrumental activities with physically disabled children, and as yet little investigated, are the effects of the rhythmic and melodic character of the music upon the motility and organization of a child's movements as he plays, and the influence of the mood of the music upon the quality and extent of his effort.

To all that music therapy may do for an individual, the group situation brings positive social experiences which reflect healthily upon him and reinforce his personal progressive developments. The mutuality of physically disabled children's pleasure in group work, and in the music they create, arises not only from the quality of the music and the instruments used but also from the manner in which instrumental arrangements are built up—the way in which each player is called upon to produce distinct, attractive parts of unified musical experiences. As the children share attentively in such music making, the quality of the enjoyment they feel in the music is directly transferred to their interpersonal relationships. Freedom from the emotional confusions of disability is induced, and an easy mood of willingness-to-try develops in the commitment of the group. All the children's musical sensibilities are activated—an experience in which many find deep personal fulfillment—and the special musical talents of individuals are given every possible chance of unfolding so that they may find expression in the group's work and add to its content of musical activity.

An effective practical method of creating an arrangement is to take such a song as "Hello!" for younger children or "Can You Sing to the Sun?" for older ones, to which a resonator bell arrangement has been made (see Chapter 2). Enjoy singing the song with the group until the children are sufficiently familiar

246

with it, and then introduce instruments one by one. Keeping the resonator bell arrangement in mind as a guide only, choose for each successive child who is to take an instrumental part an instrument he is able to play; let his part be as simple as it needs to be to suit his abilities. Repeat the song for each new player to establish him in his part with the others and to allow everyone to experience the musical addition. Make it into a musical adventure! As the arrangement builds up, try to create a contrast of instrumental sounds within a unity of mood that suits the song. Incorporate drum, tambourine, and/or cymbal parts, as appropriate. According to the response of the group, the arrangement can be evolved still further in subsequent sessions if this is musically valid.

Using the knowledge gained of the children's abilities and building on their familiarity with the instruments, create other arrangements in other moods and tempos. Let the complexity of the arrangements increase naturally out of the children's growth of ability and perceptiveness, but do not force the pace. Allow each arrangement to be enjoyed and its developmental possibilities to be explored as those children who could not originally play a particular instrument or part show the urge to try. The same principles of instrumental experimentation and substitution of parts can be applied to creating arrangements of music, other than songs, which are right for the group.

Group instrumental activities with physically disabled children will necessarily be ongoing, experimental, upbuilding; goals will change as children develop and new, unforseeable goals emerge. The reach and content of the work will evolve differently with each group, and the appropriate selection, adaptation, or composition of materials to meet any particular group's emotional requirements and various physical capacities will always be the essential basis for maintaining constructive work. The considerations of choice and content of materials in Chapter 3 are revelant here.

Appendix 2

Adapting Materials

With special thanks to: Cindy Batchelor, Kay Brockway, Eileen Hughes, Herbert and Gail Levin, Michael McGuire, Vera Moretti, Sybil Beresford-Peirse, Carol Robbins, Gendie Solloway and Aileen Stead for their contributions to this appendix.

The resources available to a therapist can be widened considerably through an active interest in adapting materials to suit her particular client group. This will broaden the repertoire on which she can draw and increase the range of experiences and activities she can realize in therapy. Reworking or modifying materials carefully to suit the abilities of a group or to fulfill a need can be truly creative. When a composer writes a song or arranges a piece for instruments for use in music therapy, he or she does this at one point in time, and usually with a particular group in mind. The piece is then published in this form. Obviously, he or she cannot know how differently the piece would have had to be written for a quite different group. This can only be discovered by the therapist working in that situation—who therefore has the right, the freedom, and the responsibility to make such a creative adaptation. In a real sense her work in suiting the piece to her group can become a living extension of the original creative impulse of the composer.

The examples in this appendix are of adaptations to Nordoff-Robbins materials, but obviously, the principles involved apply broadly to all available materials.

Instrumental Arrangements
Instrumental parts in compositions and arrangements exist to bring children or adults into experiences of active music-making. The parts

248

should have musical effect, sound interesting, be fun to play, and involve each player in a specific musical experience. However, such parts, as published, cannot be appropriate to the abilities of every group.

If the mood or content of a piece is right for a group, but the parts are too complex to be understood or played by its members, simplification must take place—otherwise the parts, instead of bringing the players into the music, will, in effect, keep them out of the music. If resourceful leading cannot enable the players to "grow into" successful experiences within the arrangement as scored—in a reasonable time period—then the scoring must be simplified.

How this is done depends to some extent on the piece itself. In *Fun for Four Drums,* for example (page 140), the rhythmic structure of the drum parts cannot be changed without radically changing the character and design of the whole piece. But the more complex parts, the various interchanges in the score between the four rhythmic ideas, can be omitted—either until the players have sufficient understanding to be able to attempt them, or permanently if these sections are beyond the group's abilities. In this case, one would accept the progress made in mastering the individual parts as sufficient gain in itself.

Sometimes it may be enough to play a piece in a slower tempo, or to play just the passages that are too rhythmically demanding for the players at half tempo—or even slower—and adapt the piano part accordingly. This can work when the piece has enough melodic/harmonic impact, or the parts are vivid enough to sustain interest. See, for example, *Fanfares and Dances,* "Take a Horn and Blow It."

You may be able to use part of an arrangement, such as the chorus section of "Swing Low, Sweet Chariot," *Folk Songs for Children to Sing and Play,* which uses only three resonator bells (or reed horns), but may find the bell part in the verse section too difficult for your group. Either omit instruments in this section and just sing it, or substitute simple soft percussion parts, perhaps cymbal and triangle. Return to the chorus section with its instruments, as written.

In arrangements for many instruments, simplify by being selective and having the instruments play less. For example, in "Kum Ba Yah" *(Spirituals)*—which is scored on a cumulative or "Bolero" principle, whereby the number of instruments playing parts increases with each verse—have the instruments play only with the verse in which they are scored to enter. When they have played, they drop out as the new instruments play in the next verse, and so forth. This will result in fewer players for the leader to coordi-

249

nate, making it easier to focus guidance on those playing. Each part will also stand out more clearly. Omit any part that is too complex, and simplify the rhythm of any part beyond the player's grasp. If necessary, concentrate on only two or three contrasting verses.

Parts themselves may be simplified very effectively. An example is "All Night, All Day" *(Spirituals)*, page 119. If the resonator bell melody in the introduction is too complex, transfer it to the piano, on the resonator bells have one player repeat an F in half notes, or one or two players alternate F's an octave apart in half notes. Simplify the bell part throughout the piece in a similar manner. Reduce the gong part to playing only at the beginning and end of the A sections. Keep the triangle part in the B section as it is, as far as possible, and concentrate on the contrasts between resonator bells, horn, and gong and between the triangle and autoharp. Simplifications call for a careful decision: what cannot be assimilated or played with comprehension can become a lifeless impediment to everyone's work. On the other hand, you do not want to cease challenging players' abilities, where this is appropriate, or to inhibit greater perception and capability from developing.

When it is necessary to adapt to a considerable extent, treat the scored arrangement as a model only. Use the original choice of instruments and the character of their parts to provide some guidelines for developing a simpler arrangement. Use the piano score as it is.

Instrumental arrangements may also be made more complex in order to stimulate and lead forward the abilities of more advanced children. One possibility is to reduce the number of players in an arrangement so that each child is carrying two, or even three parts. "Kum Ba Yah," for instance, has worked extremely well in this regard with profoundly and severely hearing impaired children of normal intelligence. Resonator bell arrangements for many players can really become challenging, when given to a few players, or possibly even to one player. One can also have the children take the responsibility in turn of directing the group, or play without direction, from memory.

A further possibility for increasing complexity is to take sections of the piano part and transfer them to instruments, to be played by the group with the scored parts. Bar instruments or the Melodica family are useful for this. A good example is found in *Fanfares and Dances*, No. 2. The ostinati in the left hand of the piano part can be transferred to bar instruments with very little change: the first ostinato in half notes may be played on a xylophone, the second ostinato in whole notes sounds well on a metallophone. Sustained tones can be very effectively played on a cello or violin, either open string or with a marked fingerboard.

Sometimes a child or adult who plays his own instrument well enough can be included in an arrangement. For example, a guitar can provide a slow accompaniment while the group is directed to play a melody such as "Edelweiss" on reed horns. A flute or clarinet might provide the melody in an arrangement of "Peace Like a River." In one performance of the *Children's Christmas Play,* given by physically handicapped, learning disabled, and emotionally disturbed children, an adolescent studying trumpet joined the piano to play a number of the carols the audience sang in the course of the play.

In using materials adaptively, the most important needs are to know one's materials and to be flexible in response to the working situation. There is the report of a therapist faced with thirty learning disabled adolescents—and the only instruments available were rhythm sticks. He gave out the sticks, divided the class into four groups and led everyone through *Fun For Four Drums,* complete as scored.

Songs

Songs can be adapted very naturally to meet the needs of different groups. If you enjoy a certain song, feel comfortable with it and want to use it, but find the words inappropriate or uninteresting for your group, there is no reason why other words should not be put to the melody.

It will be important that the new words are naturally singable with the melody, that the music's general character suits the content of the words, and that the clients do not have previous positive or significant associations with the original song.

The following examples are taken from various therapists' work, showing different kinds of adaptation.

"A Rainy Day" *(Playsongs 2)* was made into a "day and date naming song" by a student therapist, for patients in the geriatric unit of a psychiatric center. Many of the patients were often disoriented, and the song was used to focus them on the here and now. It was much enjoyed by the group.

> It's our music day,
> It's our music day,
> Today is _____(day)_____ ,
> It's our music day.

Its the _____(date)_____,
Its the _____(date)_____,
Today is _____(day)_____,
It's our music day.

A therapist found the words of "Listen to the Birds" *(Playsongs 1)* to be inappropriate for her group of inner city, learning disabled children. She and the group sang instead: "Listen to the bells as we ring them!" All the children had bells, which they were to ring only after the therapist sang "Listen!" (over a tremolo chord to match the sound of the bells). Four times the group played antiphonally with the therapist before concluding the song. "Listen to the flutes as we blow them!" and "Listen to the shakers as we shake them!" followed. The shortness of the song, its clear structure, and the immediate relationship of speech and action, held the group's limited attention. The therapist also found this adaptation good for setting limits and for instilling the concept of taking turns.

She also related "Sing a Song About a House" *(Playsongs 1)* closely to the home circumstances of a group of learning disabled fourteen-year-olds. "With pictures on the walls! And a carpet on the floor!" held little meaning for most, but they could identify with "A T.V. and a chair!" and with kitchen appliances. Catching their interest conceptually opened them to the lyricism and gentle mood of the music. They grew to love the song and it became a "stand-by" in the sessions.

"What Shall We Do?" *(Playsongs 1)*, originally written to elicit simple singing and to stimulate children to vocalize with animal sounds, was changed by the same therapist to provide a framework for individual turns at the drum. To "What will David do on the drum?", David was encouraged to beat the drum with her. In the third line she sang about how he was beating—or could beat. She then improvised in the harmonic structure of the song, leading him into developing freedom or control, confidence or awareness, as needed. The final line became: "That's how David beats on that drum!"

A dance therapist, wanting a song to get her children resting and relaxing after movement, used the "Crying Song" *(Playsongs 2)*, substituting these words:

> It's time we should be resting,
> It's time we should be resting,
> Lie down, lie down.

Later, to get them up, she sang:

> We can start to move again,
> We can start to move again,
> Stand up, stand up.

The words of "Goodbye" *(Playsongs 1)* were changed for the group of geriatrics in a psychiatric center to: "So long! So long! Oh, thank you and so long!" because some clients were upset at the thought of singing "Goodbye"—for them it carried the meaning of parting forever. The therapist also changed the melody to suit her group. The high d's were changed to lower a's (already in the harmony) to bring the song into a singing range that was comfortable for them. It also modified the mood of the song in a way that the group seemed very comfortable with.

A song can also be used with emphasis on its language content for specific behavioral objectives, or for particular educational, social, or awareness-arousing effects. This is an adaptation of the way a song is used rather than an adaptation of the song itself—though this might also be necessary for a particular group.

To heighten a group of mentally retarded adults' awareness of greetings, to help extend their use of the word "hello", to stimulate them to respond to their names, and to communicate their names, a student therapist used four songs, two of them adapted.

1. The "Good Morning Song" *(Playsongs 2)*, the words changed to "I want to say hello!" Much emphasis was placed on shaking hands with the therapist and each other—the therapist reported that clients initiated responses and that defensive clients participated.

2. "Hello" *(Playsongs 1)*, to stimulate the use of this word by imitation, and by stressing its rhythm with rhythmic sounds, resonator bells and drum. The rhythmic variety and harmonies of the song appeared to help evoke responses.

3. "Roll Call Song" *(Playsongs 2)*, clients were encouraged to identify themselves to the group and to point each other out—this was a popular activity, everyone eagerly awaited his turn.

4. "I Have A Name" *(Playsongs 1)*, adapted freely to "You have a name," or "He has a name," then "Won't you call him by his name" or "We must call you by your name," as the situation prompted. The song continued with "That's his

(your) name." Verbal clients were encouraged with "Sing your name," and the nonverbal, to "Show me your name," on their communication boards. The original spelling part of the song was irrelevant to this group and was omitted. The song appeared to work well for these goals and objectives.

Any of the Playsongs designed as teaching aids may be used to support intensive learning experiences.

One therapist used the "Color Song" *(Playsongs 4)* as a color learning game, by focussing the children's attention on differently colored musical instruments—such as a green bell, a black clave, and a red maraca placed on the floor in front of one child. The class sang "The color of the bell is green." At "I can see it with this eye," the child picked up the bell and showed it to the class. This was repeated with the other instruments and other children taking turns. The instruments were then replaced with three identically shaped blocks in the same three colors. The song was repeated with the words "The color of the block is green," and so forth. With the colors alone to guide them, the children's responses indicated if true color identification was being achieved. This game also worked well for nonverbal children.

Pictures and charts using written language and color-coding can also be used with songs for specific teaching purposes.

In work with hearing impaired children, it was standard practice to chart the words of all songs to aid the development of reading, sight vocabulary, and verbal memory. Frequently pictures were also used to bring concepts or a sequence of events more clearly to the children's minds. An example of this is the use of a chart showing successive stages of a sunrise, integrated directly with the repeating phrases and gradual crescendo of "The Sun is Rising" *(The Three Bears)*. See page 112.

For six-to-seven-year-old hearing impaired children, the simple instrumental song "We'll Make Music" *(Music for the Hearing Impaired—and Other Special Groups)* became both an instrumental activity and a learning unit on the names of the instruments. The five instruments—drum, cymbal, horn, resonator bell and tambourine—were each pictured on small laminated cards with the name beneath the picture. Work began as the players drew for their instruments by picking a card out of a small inverted drum. Each was required to communicate the name of his instrument before obtaining it. The words of the

254

song were written on sentence strips and inserted in a wall chart. Instrument cards placed in the chart indicated where each child played his part. (Such uses of wall charts, instrument cards, and sentence strips are pictured in *Music for the Hearing Impaired—and Other Special Groups*, pages 193–4 and 205). The close combining of these visual aids with the words of the song and the actual playing of the instruments made an effective educational unit.

With older citizens in a health related facility, a student therapist used the resonator bell arrangement of "A Rainy Day" *(Songs for Children with Resonator Bells)*. She prepared four pictures representing different weather conditions: sunny, snowy, rainy, and cloudy. In addition she made a color-coded chart showing the words and the bell parts in relation to them. Blanks were left for the words/ideas that were to come from the group:

It's a _____ day	What shall we do
black pink blue purple	⬤ ⬤ ⬤ ⬤
It's a _____ day	On a _____ day?
red brown yellow green	⬤ ⬤ ⬤ ⬤
We'll _____	That's what we'll do
⬤ ⬤ ⬤ ⬤	⬤ ⬤ ⬤ ⬤
On a _____ day	On a _____ day.
⬤ ⬤ ⬤ ⬤	⬤ ⬤ ⬤ ⬤

(The sequence of colors is the same in each section of the chart, the coding being: black F#″, pink E″, blue D″, purple C#″, red B′, brown A′, yellow G′, green F#′.)

Each resonator bell was coded with a matching colored disc.

The activity began with a member of the group being asked to look out of the window and select the picture that best corresponded to the weather. The same person was asked what she or he might like to do on such a day. The answer and suggestion were inserted in the appropriate slots in the chart. The bells and mallets were given out to the players, each being asked to identify the color of the disc on his bell and to find its mate on the chart. As necessary, instruction was given on reading the chart and on following the therapist's chart-pointing. The group's playing was usually practiced initially without the music. With this group it was necessary to change the eighth notes in the bell part (they were too fast for the group to coordinate smoothly) to dotted quarters. Pauses were left in the accompaniment to accommodate this. When the group was ready, the bells and music were put together for a successful experience. All group members were encouraged to sing along by reading the chart.

Plays

Adaptations are often necessary in producing plays, for a variety of reasons. Among them may be the abilities of those taking roles, the number of players available, the length of time available for rehearsals or performance, or the nature of the facilities available for production.

It is usually possible to omit sections of a play if narration is used to connect. This should be done so that the mood of the play is maintained. Narration with, or alternating with, suitable music can be helpful in achieving this. Sometimes, the music can be taken from the play itself.

For one production of *The Children's Christmas Play* it was necessary to shorten the play because of the limited time that children could be available for performance. This was done by omitting all of the opening action and the music from page 8 of the score through the middle of page 15. "Mary and Joseph's Music" was then adapted to structure the four key lines of narration and the entrances of the characters. After the opening carol, "O Come, All Ye Faithful," the Narrator spoke his first line:

"Many, many years ago, in Bethlehem, there lived a Farmer. It was wintertime." As the Farmer entered with his animals, three children with bells and the pianist played the first five measures of "Mary and Joseph's Music." The Narrator spoke his second line:

"Three Kings came along the road to Bethlehem. They were following a star and carrying gifts in their hands." The next five measures of the music were played as the Kings entered and

256

remained off to one side. The Narrator spoke the third line:

"There were three Shepherds. They were tired and were looking for a place to sleep." During the next five measures of the music, the Shepherds entered, found their places and went to sleep. The Narrator spoke his fourth line:

"Then came Joseph, and with him was his wife, Mary, riding on a donkey." To the remaining eight measures of the music, Mary, Joseph, and the Donkey entered and took their positions, ready to begin the next scene by looking for a place to stay.

The alternation of the Narrator's lines and the music had a structuring, dignifying effect. The warm, gentle quality of the music set the mood of the entrances and the opening of the play. The movement and development of the music, from phrase to phrase, gave a feeling of progression to the action.

One therapist adapted *The Children's Christmas Play* very freely to suit the exacting demands of her emotionally disturbed and autistic children. She used only what was helpful from the staging, speech and music in the published score, and included other appropriate songs important to the children. She worked toward a production tailored closely around her children's needs and abilities. The play evolved in particular ways from year to year as individual children developed or moved on to other roles. In the Finale "Christmas Bells," she changed the words (and the melodic rhythm as necessary) beginning in measure 9 to:—

> Happy Christmas to you all,
> From us all at ＿＿＿＿＿＿＿＿ School.
> From us all at ＿＿＿＿＿＿＿＿ School,
> Joy! Joy! Joy! Joy!

—then continuing to the end of the song as written. She felt that this change brought the children closer to sharing the Christmas message of joy with the audience. Sometimes these lines were sung by all the children, at times by one child courageous enough to sing solo.

In contrast to these extensive adaptations, her productions of the play with physically disabled children and youths, mostly of normal intelligence, followed the published score exactly— except for additions made to suit the group. One performance opened with a colorful peal of large bells. These were rung by a severely quadriplegic boy whose handicaps made it impossible for him to take an acting role or to handle other instruments. He was given the responsibility of ringing a number of Greek mule and goat bells suspended from a bar to make this dramatic beginning to the play. (See *Creative Music Therapy*, page 213, for photographs of a similar use of such bells.) He also joined in the free ringing of bells in the closing measures of the Finale. Because of the size of the auditorium, and the slow pace of the Kings as they walked through it, the therapist extended "Three Kings Journeying" by inserting "Personent Hodie" ("Sing Aloud on This Day!"), using the arrangement by Gustav Holst. The seriousness and affirmative strength of this music was most suitable at this moment in the play—it also blended in well with the music in the score and with the carols.

Considerations relevant to the adapting of plays will be found in *Chapter Four:* Plays with Music, and also in *Therapy in Music for Handicapped Children,* pages 22–23, 84–86, and 120–124.

Appendix 3

Reed Horns: Their Use and Maintenance

An outfit of reed horns comprises four "Acme" horns complete with pitch-pipe holders, and a set of sixteen "Kratt" pitch-pipes sounding every tone chromatically from E′ to G″.

To prepare a horn for use: Unscrew the mouthpiece and then the cap of the pitch-pipe holder—make sure the holder is screwed firmly into the horn body. Open the box of pitch-pipes by squeezing in the sides at the end away from the hinge and lifting the top. Insert the selected tone in the holder so that the end of the pitch-pipe on which the tone letter is shown goes in last. Screw the cap on securely and replace the mouthpiece. The horn is now ready for use.

To produce a full even tone, place the end of the mouthpiece within the lips (not against them) and blow the horn firmly but without a strong attack. If a horn is blown too forcefully, the pressure of the breath will "pin the reed down," blocking the air passage and immobilizing the reed, preventing the horn from blowing.

The higher tones are easy to sound and it is recommended that children with undeveloped breath control begin with these. Below G′ the horns require more care in blowing and provide a good exercise in sustaining breath control.

For ready identification of the tone of a horn affix a small self-adhesive label inside the bell. When the horn is fitted with a pitch-pipe write the tone on the label—this will be helpful when giving horns out or when directing. When a horn tone is changed, erase the former tone and write in the new.

The pitch-pipes have been specially tuned for the horns, they should not be used for tuning purposes out of the horns for they will then sound sharp—particularly the higher tones.

Cleaning the Horns

For normal daily use, clean the mouthpiece with Zephiran Chloride in a 1:750 dilution (available from most drugstores). Simply moisten a cloth with the solution and wipe the mouthpiece.

After some months of regular use, remove the mouthpieces, the pitch-pipe holders and caps, and boil for a few minutes. Immerse the pitch-pipes in a strong antiseptic such as Lysol for an hour or so. Rinse, dry and reassemble. Some therapists soak all the parts that come into contact with the breath in Tarnex or a similar metal cleaning preparation to maintain freshness. The horn body will need only washing in warm soapy water.

Tuning the Horns

Usually the reeds keep their pitch indefinitely, but at times, after extensive or energetic use, they may go out of tune. This is a simple matter to remedy. The reed is mounted on a brass plate and housed inside the silver tube of the pitch-pipe. Slip the brass plate out of the tube by pushing a thin pen or similar object against the end that shows the tone letter. Set the plate at the edge of a table with the reed uppermost, and the end showing the tone letter over the edge of the table.

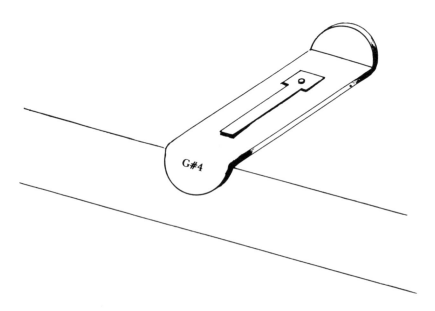

To support the reed, slip the blade of knife between the reed and the brass plate.

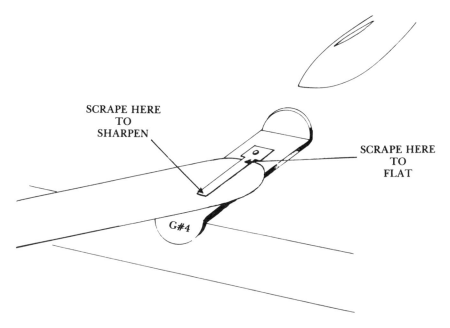

SCRAPE HERE
TO
SHARPEN

SCRAPE HERE
TO
FLAT

G#4

Use a *sharp* knife to scrape the reed *lightly* to remove a *minute* amount of metal:
> Scraping the free end of the reed will sharpen the pitch. Scraping near the rivet, where the reed flexes as it vibrates, will lower the pitch—the lightest scrape here can change the pitch.

If you prefer, fine emery paper may be used in place of the knife. Insert the reed back in the tube, the end showing the tone goes in first. Fit the pitch-pipe in the horn before testing the pitch.

Occasionally, a horn becomes difficult to blow. This is usually the result of overenergetic use. The reed has been pressed too close to the plate, cutting off the air flow necessary for it to vibrate. Remove the reed plate, as for tuning, and gently lever up the reed with a knife until a small gap is created and the horn blows easily. Do not open the gap too wide as this will give a poor tone quality.

Appendix 4

Music Therapy for Children — Literature and Resources

Reference Literature

Alvin, J. *Music for Handicapped Children*. New York: Oxford University Press, 1965.

Alvin, J. *Music Therapy*. New York: Oxford University Press, 1966.

Bailey, P. *They Can Make Music*. New York: Oxford University Press, 1973.

Birkenshaw, L. *Music for Fun, Music for Learning*. Toronto: Holt, Rinehart and Winston of Canada Ltd., 1974. Revised 3rd Edition 1983 (U.S. distributor: Magnamusic-Baton).

Bitcon, C. *Alike and Different*. Santa Ana: Rosha Press, 1976.

Clark, C. and Chadwick, D. *Clinically Adapted Instruments for the Multiply Handicapped*. Magnamusic-Baton, St. Louis, MO.

Dobbs, J.P.B. *The Slow Learner and Music*. New York: Oxford University Press, 1966.

Graham, R. (Ed.) *Music for the Exceptional Child*. Reston, Virginia: Music Educators National Conference, 1975.

Nocera, S. *Reaching the Special Learner Through Music*. Morristown, New Jersey: Silver Burdett Company, 1980.

Nordoff, P. and Robbins, C. *Music Therapy for the Handicapped Child*. London: Gollancz, 1971 (U.S. distributor: Belwin Mills)

Nordoff, P. and Robbins, C. *Creative Music Therapy*. New York: John Day Company (Harper and Row), 1977.

Pratt, R. and Peterson, M. *Elementary Music for All Learners*. Sherman Oaks, California: Alfred Publishing Company, Inc., 1981.

Schulberg, C. *Music Therapy Sourcebook*. Human Sciences Press, NY 1981.

Robbins, C. and Robbins, C. *Music for the Hearing Impaired—and Other Special Groups*. St. Louis, Missouri: Magnamusic-Baton, Inc., 1980.

Ward, D. *Hearts and Hands and Voices*. New York: Oxford University Press, 1976.

Zimmer, . *Music Handbook for the Child in Special Education*. European American Music Dist. 1976, Totowa, NJ.

Materials Especially Composed for Group Activities by the Authors

Pif-Paf-Poltrie
The First Book of Children's Play-Songs
The Second Book of Children's Play-Songs
The Third Book of Children's Play-Songs
The Fourth Book of Children's Play-Songs
The Fifth Book of Children's Play-Songs
The Three Bears
The Story of Artaban
Fun For Four Drums
The Children's Christmas Play
Spirituals for Children to Sing and Play
Children's Play Play-Songs with Resonator Bells
The Twenty-Third Psalm
Fanfares and Dances
A Message for the King
Folk Songs for Children to Sing and Play
Some Prayers From the Ark

Published by Theodore Presser Company, Bryn Mawr, Pennsylvania 19010.
European distributor: Alfred A. Kalmus Ltd. 2/3 Fareham St., London W.1

Materials Especially Composed by Herbert and Gail Levin

Learning Through Music (Levin, Levin and Safer)
Learning Through Song (Levin, Levin and Safer)

Published by Teaching Resources Company, 50 Pond Park Road, Hingham, Massachusetts 02043

A Garden of Bell Flowers
Learning Songs

Published by Theodore Presser Company, Bryn Mawr, Pennsylvania 19010

Autoharp Instruction Books and Materials

Catalog available from M.P. Enterprises, Box 454, Summit, New Jersey 07901

Appendix 5

Suppliers of Special Instruments

Sets of Bird Calls and Reed Horns

Sole U.S. Distributor

MMB Music, Inc.
3526 Washington Avenue
St. Louis, MO 63103-1019

Great Britain

London Music Shop
39–45 Coldharbour Lane
London S.E.5 9NR
England

Chordal Dulcimer, Pentatonic Zither (Goldilocks), Diatonic Zither, Nordic Lyre

Obtaining these instruments is now problematic as the company previously manufacturing them no longer exists. However, it is possible to make such instruments. Instructions will be found in: *Musical Instruments Made to Be Played*, by Ronald Roberts. Dryad Press, P.O. Box 38, Northgates, Leicester LE1 9BU, England.

Toy Harp—The Golden Junior Harp, and Zithers

Department stores, toy shops, or direct from the manufacturer:

Harbert Italiano S.A.S.
20157 Milano
Via Eritrea 19
Italy

Lyres

Sophia Ltd.
William Morris Yard
Forest Row, East Sussex
England

Several models are in production including a 12 string penta-tonic lyre suitable for "Goldilocks" in *The Three Bears*. Catalog available on request.

Resonator Bells and Replacement Beaters

Especially Recommended: Tone Educator Bells
Distributed by: Lyons, Inc.
530 Riverview Avenue
Elkhart, Indiana 46514
Also: STUDIO 49 Resonator Bells
Distributed by: MMB Music, Inc.
3526 Washington Avenue
St. Louis, MO 63103-1019
Also: Sonor Resonator Bells
Distributed by: M. Hohner, Inc.
Andrews Road
Hicksville, L.I., N.Y. 11802

Handchimes

Attractive, ingenious instruments, played much the same way as handbells but requiring very little skill. The sound is comparable to good quality resonator bells. A useful resource for the physically disabled or blind.

The Handchime Company Ltd.
Court Street
Moretonhampstead, Newton Abbot,
Devon, England, TQ13 8NA

available in the U.S. from:
Schulmerich Carillons
Carillon Hill
Sellersville, Pennsylvania 18960

Handbells

Schulmerich Carillons
Carillon Hill
Sellersville, Pennsylvania 18960

available in the U.K. from:
The Handchime Company Ltd.
Court Street
Moretonhampstead,
Newton Abbot,
Devon, England, TQ13 8NA

Greek Bells

These bells are sold by weight (per kilo) and are made in many Greek towns. We have obtained bells from:

Costas Balakosta, Bell Maker
Karditsa
Greece

INDEX